3/6

ECUMENICAL STUDIES IN HISTORY
No. 5

# THE SIGNIFICANCE
# OF
# SOUTH INDIA

by

MICHAEL HOLLIS

*formerly Moderator of the
Church of South India*

LUTTERWORTH PRESS

LONDON

# ECUMENICAL STUDIES IN HISTORY

The purpose of this series is to examine afresh problems of Church History and to do this for the sake of Church Unity. The subjects are drawn from many periods, places and communions. Their unity lies not in a common outlook of the writers, nor in a common method of treatment. It lies solely in the aim of, in one way or another, directly or indirectly, furthering the unity of the Church. The contributors are no less diverse than the subjects, and represent many Churches, nations and races.

## General Editors

THE REV. A. M. ALLCHIN, Pusey House, Oxford.
THE REV. MARTIN E. MARTY, PH.D., University of Chicago.
THE REV. T. H. L. PARKER, D.D., Oakington Vicarage, Cambridge.

## Advisory Board

In grateful affection
to
J. S. M. HOOPER
to whom both I personally and the whole
Church of South India owe more than can
be measured or expressed

Lutterworth Press

4 Bouverie Street, London, E.C.4


John Knox Press

Richmond, Virginia, U.S.A.


*Printed in Great Britain by*
*Latimer Trend & Co Ltd, Plymouth*

# CONTENTS

# INTRODUCTION

THE AIM of this book is not to compare in detail the various other Plans for bringing about a united Church with what was done in South India. There are too many of them and they are at many different stages and liable to alteration. In any case, to do it usefully would call for far more space and for the kind of treatment which Dr. Sundkler gave in his book on the Church of South India. Often the most interesting thing is not the final form but the stages through which it came to be, the various arguments and pressures, the tentative suggestions and the reasons which caused them to be rejected or modified. That demands close study of unpublished documents and, if possible, contact with those immediately responsible.

Rather, I have taken certain broad developments in South India and seen how they have affected later attempts in other situations to get a united Church started. Maybe something will result which is useful for those who are still looking for an agreed way and perhaps I can call attention to questions which need to be thought about if we are to go forward. I must make plain that this is not an official book and that the Church of South India is in no way responsible for anything in it.

There is a sense in which South India was extraordinarily fortunate. From the beginning the negotiators included a number of exceptionally able men, some nationals and some foreigners, drawn from all the Churches concerned. The Constitution which they produced has needed remarkably little alteration and no major changes. I can speak freely because it was all in its final shape before I had any share in the negotiations. There was most thorough examination of all that was suggested both in India and outside. There was full consultation with Church leaders and scholars in many parts of the world. But the negotiators and other leaders in the Indian Churches concerned were never overawed by Western theologians or ecclesiastics. They paid attention to what was said but they exercised their own judgment and came to their own conclusions. For this India was better equipped than some other areas where union negotiations have taken place.

I would like to sum up my own feelings about C.S.I. First, there is the release from the bondage of the past. It is not that history ceases to matter, but that it ceases to dominate. All the Western Churches, with centuries of existence behind them, have the same tendency to look back and, by an appeal to precedent, to seek to avoid answering radically new questions. To quote an example from the Report of the Committee of the Lambeth Conference of 1948 which dealt with the Church of South India: "We have never yet entered into full communion with any Church which does not possess a fully unified ministry, episcopally ordained."[1] This was taken then, and is apparently still looked upon today, as closing the issue. There is no trace in any of the various union negotiations that Anglicans have been asked, or have asked themselves, whether the time may have come for them to do what they have never done, in order that God may begin to heal the divisions among His people. After all, when Peter said, "Not so, Lord; for I have never . . ." he found that the Holy Spirit made it clear that this was no sufficient answer.[2]

There is not only this refusal to face new questions, on the apparent assumption that the old answers are final. There is the more disturbing tendency to avoid certain issues because they are too dangerous. The continued existence of the Church of England, or of the Anglican Communion, is treated as so important that decision on certain controversial points is impossible. My comment, after experience of C.S.I., is twofold. First, no one knows the power of the Holy Spirit to guide into deeper understanding until he has taken part in really serious seeking of God's way to unity, built upon a certainty that unity is what God wants. The West has become so accustomed to our present denominationalism, which is beyond any question not what our Lord prayed for, that it forgets who prayed that those who believe on Him may be one, as He and the Father are one, that the world may believe that the Father has sent Him. Unity becomes rather an ideal than the plain purpose and will of God. Even Anglicans can be led into a common mind, if they will seek it with their fellow Christians in the context of Christ's prayer for a visible unity. Secondly, if preserving the Church of England, or the Anglican Communion, is to be taken as in practice the final aim, when it may be that it has in its present form done what it

[1] *Lambeth 1948*, p. 46 (part ii).
[2] Acts 10: 14.

can do and is even ripe to disappear, then it has ceased to be an instrument in God's hand and become an idol. No denomination has final validity.

There is in much of Western Christianity a strange absence of any sense of urgency. It is too easily assumed that, if union comes, it will come so slowly that few if any alive today will see it. The policies of all the major denominations unconsciously presuppose that they have a generation or more of separate existence to plan for. They build up institutions, they debate problems, in an isolation which makes no sense if disunity is to be overcome. I know how my predecessor as Bishop of Madras refused to make plans for developments which would have been highly desirable, or even essential, if Anglicanism were to continue as a separate entity, because he was determined not to make the coming of unity in South India more difficult. I see very little evidence of that kind of thinking in Britain. Yet, if disunity is really contrary to the known will of God and a serious hindrance to His purpose of reconciliation for the world, it ought to call out our full energies, with compelling urgency, so that the search for God's way to the kind of unity for which Christ prayed takes a major place in our prayers, our thinking and planning and in all use of our resources in personnel and funds.

Finally, is it wrong to hope for more understanding of the position of those who have elsewhere been closely engaged in negotiations for unity or who have lived within a united Church? Too little use is made of their experience when unity is under discussion. There are those, in every country and from every denominational tradition, who could give much if they were allowed to do so. But they cannot just repeat the old denominational shibboleths. How can one who, as I have done, has for thirteen years lived in fellowship with colleagues, some episcopally ordained and some not, without discovering any essential difference in God's working, look upon the problem of the various ministries quite like someone who has never moved outside the denominational walls? In the last of my seven years as bishop of the C.S.I. diocese of Madras, out of 93 presbyters barely one-third had been episcopally ordained and the proportion in 1947 was much lower. It is not good enough to declare that God cannot do something, while refusing to look at the evidence that He is doing it all the time.

The scope of this study is intentionally limited. I have not tried to follow out the effect of the C.S.I. on the Lutherans, because that is something which deserves a book on its own. I would only call the attention of those interested to articles in various numbers of the *Lutheran World*. If I seem to have said much about Anglican reactions to C.S.I., that is because they have put so much more in print and because they have found more difficulties about what has been done and is being done in South India. I have also, inevitably, with my Anglican background and being now again within the Church of England, more contact with what is taking place in it.

It would have been much easier if there were in Britain anything comparable to the Ecumenical Library in Union Theological Seminary, New York. The absence in Britain of even one fully equipped centre for the study of the movement for Christian unity, with a proper supply of books and papers and a staff that could direct reading and study, is an indication that British Christianity does not yet take its disunity seriously enough. We are not really unhappy about what we too easily call our unhappy divisions—not unhappy as our Lord is unhappy.

# LITERATURE

FOR SOUTH INDIA:

*The Church of South India*, Sundkler, Lutterworth Press. (Quoted as Sundkler.)

*The Constitution of the Church of South India, with the Basis of Union.* C.L.S. Madras and Lutterworth Press, London, 1952. (Quoted as *C.* or *BU.*)

*Church of South India. The Book of Common Worship.* O.U.P., London, 1963.

Copies of the *Synod Minutes* may be found with the major Missionary Societies. (Quoted as *Synod* with date.)

*Agreed Statements*, ed. J. R. Chandran, C.L.S., Madras, 1960. (Quoted as *Agreed Statements.*)

*The Reunion of the Church*, J. E. L. Newbigin, 2nd ed. with a new preface, S.C.M. Press, London, 1960. His criticisms of the actions of the Lambeth Conference, 1958, and of proposals for an act of unification of the ministries of uniting Churches by a service including the laying on of hands have not, in my opinion, been adequately answered.


FOR NORTH INDIA/PAKISTAN:

The handiest form of the texts is *Ceylon North India Pakistan* edited by Bishop Stephen Bayne, Jr., S.P.C.K., London, 1960. Some important changes have been made since that date. The Fourth (revised) edition is now available from C.L.S., Madras, or Lutterworth Press.

Any serious study calls for use of the quarterly magazine *Church Union News and Views*, published in India.

An important article by one deeply concerned with the negotiations is: *The North India-Pakistan Proposals for Unification* by William Stewart, *Ecumenical Review*, Vol. XV, No. 2, Jan. 1963.

FOR CEYLON

The texts are in Bishop Bayne's book but here again there have been developments.

D. T. Niles has an important article *Church Union in North India, Pakistan and Ceylon* in *Ecumenical Review*, Vol. XIV, No. 3, April 1962.

FOR AUSTRALIA

*The Faith of the Church* (1959) and *The Church: Its Nature, Function and Ordering* (1963) are available through the Lutterworth Press, London. The article by Professor J. D. McCaughey in *Ecumenical Review*, Vol. XVII, No. 1, Jan. 1965, called *Church Union in Australia*, should be consulted.

Other Plans may be available with the Missionary Societies concerned with the areas involved or in libraries.

A brief source of information, indicating where documents may be obtained, is *Christian Unity and the Anglican Communion*, a survey by David M. Paton and R. M. C. Jeffrey, Church Information Office, Church House, Westminster, S.W.1., but, as the title shows, this is limited in scope.

*The Lutheran World* is published quarterly from 150 route de Ferney, 1211 Geneva 20, Switzerland.

CONFERENCE REPORTS

*Lambeth Conference 1948*, S.P.C.K., London. (Quoted as *Lambeth 1948*.)

*Lambeth Conference 1958*. S.P.C.K., London, and Seabury Press. (Quoted as *Lambeth 1958*.)

*The Fourth World Conference on Faith and Order* is the report of the conference at Montreal, 1963, ed. Rodger and Vischer, S.C.M. Press, London. (Quoted as *Montreal*.)

*Unity Begins at Home* is the report of the First British Faith and Order Conference at Nottingham, 1964, ed. Davies and Edwards, S.C.M. Press, London. (Quoted as *Nottingham*.)

*Documents on Christian Unity*, ed. G. K. A. Bell, O.U.P.

I *A Selection 1920–1930*.

III *1931–1947*.

IV *1948–1957*. (Quoted as Bell, *Documents*.)

The library in Britain most likely to have books, pamphlets and magazines is at Selly Oak, Birmingham.

In U.S.A. the Ecumenical Library in connection with Union Theological Seminary, New York, has almost everything.

## ACKNOWLEDGEMENTS

Thanks are due to C.L.S. (Madras) for permission to publish extracts from books of which it holds the copyright.

The extract from the Report on the Anglican-Methodist Conversations (published jointly by the Church Information Office and the Epworth Press, price 3/6d) is printed with the permission of the holders of the copyright.

# I

## THE IMPORTANCE OF SOUTH INDIA

"THE MOST IMPORTANT event in Church History since Pentecost." Exaggeration, sentimentality, near-blasphemy, illumination—so different people will judge this remark. What matters now is that it could have been made. Something was done in St. George's Cathedral, Madras, on the morning of September 27, 1947, about which no responsible Christian can be indifferent. In the words spoken by Bishop Chirakarottu Korula Jacob, presiding at the service of Inauguration,

"Dearly beloved brethren, in obedience to the Lord Jesus Christ, the Head of the Church, Who, on the night of His Passion, prayed that His Disciples might be one; and by the authority of the governing bodies of the uniting Churches, whose resolutions have been read in your hearing and laid in prayer before Almighty God; I do hereby declare that these three Churches, namely:
> the Madras, Travancore and Cochin, Tinnevelly and Dornakal Dioceses of the Church of India, Burma and Ceylon;
> the Madras, Madura, Malabar, Jaffna, Kannada, Telugu and Travancore Church Councils of the South India United Church; and
> the Methodist Church in South India, comprising the Madras, Trichinopoly, Hyderabad and Mysore Districts;
are become one

### CHURCH OF SOUTH INDIA,

and that those bishops, presbyters, deacons and probationers who have assented to the basis of Union and accepted the Constitution of the Church of South India and whose names are laid upon this holy table, are bishops, presbyters and deacons in this Church: in the name of the Father, and of the Son, and of the Holy Spirit. Amen."

Not only did something happen then. So far from being a "pantomime horse", the Church of South India is today an undeniable fact,

15

vigorous, increasingly aware of its God-given unity, and concerned that that unity should become more creative and more all-embracing. Whatever criticisms have been or may be levelled against the way in which this union was brought about; whatever inadequacies or errors some have found in its faith or order; there is today in South India one Church, where in 1947 there were three. Some believed that it was a house built in such defiance of all sound ecclesiastical principles that it would inevitably fall to pieces. There were even those who asserted that they prayed for its collapse. If so, that prayer shows no sign of being answered. The Scheme of Union put out in 1941 and implemented in 1947 has worked. It has resulted in a United Church. By that fact it demands attention. The aeroplane which flies is thereby better than one, however perfect in theory, which never got beyond the drawing-board.

This is not to say that there are no other United Churches, even if Anglicans, not being themselves involved, tend sometimes to forget the fact. They exist in North America, Asia and Africa. Nor is it true that they are only the drawing together of bodies already within the same ecclesiastical tradition. The most striking example is the United Church of Canada. But there are two barriers which have not been overcome elsewhere—the barrier of Order, which has kept Anglicans in isolation from the other Churches which also spring, in their present form, from the Reformation; and the barrier of Faith, which, particularly in the Lutheran tradition, is embodied in the great Confessions. Those formerly Anglicans made up about half the original membership of the Church of South India. There and for them an effective answer has been discovered. Ten years of Conversations with the representatives of five Lutheran Churches have made possible the initiation of actual negotiations for a United Church into which both the present Church of South India and the Lutheran Churches will die in order that God may bring into being something nearer His will than are any of them in their present separation. These are striking facts which demand to be taken seriously by all responsible Christians everywhere.

*There and for them* an effective answer has been discovered. C.S.I. has always insisted that what was done in South India cannot just be transferred elsewhere ready-made. It is not a universal blue-print for Church unity. Basically that is because unity is not something to be brought about by Schemes or Plans. There must be more than a reconciling of systems, whether they be systems of doctrine or systems of administration. The reconciliation which God has effected in Christ, which the Church exists to evidence to the world, is a reconciliation of persons. Men and women must become aware of this reconciliation and of this calling, must feel the horror of their disunity, must realize God's unhappiness at their divisions, and must be prepared themselves to pay the price without which visible unity is unattainable. No one else can do it for them.

But this truth that any reconciliation worth paying for is a reconciliation of real people, with all that they are and all that has made them what they are, demands that local facts are taken seriously. Christian disunity, in any area, is so intimately bound up with the pecularities of the history of that area that it can only be dealt with by the people of that area. Real judgments are judgments in particular circumstances, made by the people in those circumstances, who will have to deal with the consequences of their judgments. In South India we were not called on to deal with the question of two kinds of bishops, as they are in North India. We were not called on to find an answer to the difference between the paedobaptist and the upholder of believers' baptism. Both in North India, Pakistan, and in Ceylon, they are faced with that problem. The Scheme for South India was a real scheme just because it dealt with the real issues and actual possibilities found in South India at a particular time. At other times, and in other places, other Christians must discover what God has to say to them about their problems, and what solutions He will show to them.

There have been and still are critics who assert that, in certain respects, the Scheme was radically unsound and that the resultant Church is one with which it is improper to have any fellowship. Obviously the experience of eighteen years has blunted the edge of a number of these condemnations and has led to a change of mind on the part of some who were at first doubtful or openly hostile. Yet there still remain those who are convinced that there is no true advance along the lines of the Church of South India and that those who entered its fellowship did so at the cost of abandoning some essential element of the Church's true being, whether in Faith or in Order. It is not difficult to show that some of these criticisms are based on ignorance of what the Constitution of the Church of South India actually says and of what happens within the Church. Others reflect that deep-rooted human objection to change, largely irrational and especially powerful when matters of religious observance and phraseology are concerned. Ecclesiastically no less than politically, it is now all "one world". The old comfortable feeling that India was a long way off and that what "the natives" did could not affect what was done in one's own country and in one's own home church has given way to the often disturbing realization that the Church of South India challenges all Christians everywhere. It is easy to rationalize dislike of possible changes in terms of theological arguments. Yet there are serious criticisms and it is important, from the other side, not to make an idol of the South India Scheme or of any other plan for unity. Satan will certainly fight against any union plan which is in accordance with God's will. That is not to say that all union plans are in accordance with God's will or that any of them are immune from error.

It is also true that the Scheme which has issued in the Church of South India must not be looked at simply as a document. It has done its work in making possible a life in unity for Christians who were previously divided into three separately organized bodies. In the course of that life in unity they have learnt many things which they did not—and, one may confidently assert, could not—know while they were still in their separation. The history of the years since 1947 is vital to any judgment on the validity of the Scheme. It has made it possible for C.S.I. to learn more of God and His will, more of the power of the Holy Spirit and of the primacy of mission, more too of the reality of human sin and of its own shortcomings. Again, the value both to C.S.I. and to the Lutherans of ten years of Theological Conversations is incalculable; their effects can be seen far beyond South India. The enrichment of worship and, most of all, the production of the C.S.I. Order for the Lord's Supper, are fruits of our coming together which no one at the time of the Inauguration foresaw. The C.S.I. Ordinal may prove equally important for Churches all over the world. C.S.I. knows far more—and has helped others to know more—about episcopacy than the negotiators and the separate Churches which they represented did when they stated: "Some regard episcopacy merely as a form of church government which has persisted in the Church through the centuries and may as such be called historic, and which at the present time is expedient for the Church in South India. Others believe that episcopacy is of divine appointment, and that episcopal ordination is an essential guarantee of the sacraments of the Church. Some, again, hold various views intermediate between these two."[1] None of them hold today precisely what they thought they believed twenty years ago. All these insights and experiences, made possible because the Church of South India was inaugurated on this Basis of Union and

[1] *BU*, p. 76.

with this Constitution, are now potentially the possession of all the Churches everywhere. Full use has not been made of them; but the marks of what has taken place in South India are, in greater or lesser degree, to be seen in every plan and behind every plan for Christian unity. Further, the success, even if a limited success, of the seeking for unity there, has given stimulus and encouragement to those who seek unity elsewhere. Denominational structures, however resistant, however ancient, are not beyond the power of God to deal with. The Church situation can never again be just what it was before September 27, 1947.

## II

## LINES OF ADVANCE

IN ALL those Plans which promise to bring about a united Church in a foreseeable future, which means in plans concerned with actual Christians in concrete situations at this moment, there are certain common features. Utopias are unprofitable and can too easily distract men from the immediate demand for obedience here and now. A study of the events which led up to the inauguration of the Church of South India in 1947 shows how these features only became plain in the course of the negotiations. They were not the invention of those concerned, but in the different editions of the Scheme they gradually found expression, and it was in the search for God's way to an actual union that they crystallized out. It is worth while reminding the negotiators of today and tomorrow that what may seem to them obvious has only come to appear obvious because others have walked that way before them.

Just why different people agreed that advance along these lines was possible is not always easy to say. Motives are mixed, and may often be obscure, even to the persons concerned. It may well be that fuller understanding and the discovery of the right reason for certain acts can only come after we have done them. It is not possible for men to act only on certainties, and the great decisions of life are, in fact, acts of faith, whether in men or in God. So, in matters of Christian unity, there may be a pragmatic approach, where someone sees that only in a certain way is there, in the circumstances and given the people negotiating together, any hope of progress. This may be no more than a recognition of the unconquerable obstinacy of other negotiating Churches. It may be done with the definite hope that life in union will, as it does, make them more open to new ideas. It is important to distinguish between this as meaning only ideas new to the obstinate, with the unexamined assumption that the old ideas of the speaker are right and must ultimately prevail, and the more fruitful recognition that all concerned must accept the possibility that God has something really

20

new to teach them. There may be a conviction that comes about through the enriching and enlightening experience of fellowship in negotiation—a fellowship of worship, study and discussion in which people become friends at a deeper level than ever before. Here God can make new understandings and the restatement of old understandings possible, just because all are seeking a new way of obedience. The extent of mutual ignorance, even among Church leaders, is amazing, more particularly to anyone who has lived outside the dividing walls of the denominations.

The first line of advance is open when all have come to see that unity cannot mean the absorption by one Church, which remains basically unchanged, of all the others. This may seem obvious now; though experience shows that it is not so, at least wherever there is a marked discrepancy in numbers, wealth or social prestige between different organized Christian bodies. It took Anglicans, first in India, and then at the Lambeth Conference of 1930, a considerable time to realize that the Church of South India would not, and could not, be a part of the Anglican communion. Even in England today there is far too much talk, on both sides, of Methodists "returning" to the Church of England. One of the great contributions which Bishop Palmer made, both to South India and to the whole movement for Christian unity, was his insistence that dying to live is as true of the separate denominations as it is of the individual Christian.

Secondly, there is, at least among those responsible for leadership in the Churches, an agreement that the Church exists because God wants it for the sake of the world. There has developed a new apprehension of Mission. It is because God so loved *the world* that he sent His son, and because God so loved *the world* that His Son sends His disciples and gives them the Holy Spirit. This agreement does not mean that the mass of Christians and all congregations are yet aware of this truth. Too often they are inward-looking and indifferent to their responsibility towards the world. That is true not only of the West and its overseas extensions, heirs of post-Constantinian Christendom, but of the third and fourth generation Christians of Asia and Africa. Western missions have too successfully reproduced the patterns and problems of Western Christianity. Yet there can be no useful approach to the problem of unity among Christians which does not start from a deep concern for Mission, for the making known to the world that reconciliation of the world which God brought about in Christ. That concern is embodied in every Plan of Union. If we seek unity for the wrong reasons, we shall inevitably seek it in the wrong way and what we find will not be the unity for which our Lord prayed. The wrong kind of unity may be even worse than our present disunity and, so far as the making known of the gospel is concerned, may do more harm than good.

Thirdly, the necessity for an ordered ministry is accepted and, for varying reasons, there is general agreement that episcopacy must be one element in that ministry in a united Church. This may be no more than a recognition that Churches already having bishops will not give them up, but it is often more than this—a conviction that pastoral oversight exercised by a person is needed for the life of the Church. A most interesting appearance of this desire for bishops is the plan for a united Church in Australia with bishops in the historic succession, for none of the Churches involved have them.[1] The appearance of what is, in certain respects, a new pattern of episcopacy within the Church of South India has had a good deal to do with the breaking down of old prejudices and it is noteworthy that the most effective exponents of the true value of episcopacy, as it is being experienced within C.S.I., have themselves come from those traditions which have not in the past had bishops.

Fourthly, it is accepted that there must be no attempt to impose uniformity of worship as a condition of entrance into a united Church. The old battles between the upholders of freedom and those who sought to insist on the use of a liturgical form have become obsolete. The real measure of responsibility which must rest upon each congregation with its pastor for the ordering of its worship is recognized not only in C.S.I. but in all plans for union. Together with this go the necessary provisions for mutual consultation and the working out of richer patterns which may the better express our life in unity. How far the theological implications of this recognition of the necessity for variety and of the inevitability of congregational freedom are grasped is uncertain. At least there is a realization that the worship of the Church ought to express the whole inheritance of all the centuries everywhere, and that the ordering and development of the worship of a united Church must be left to grow out of its life in unity.

Fifthly, there is the recognition that union cannot be brought about either by the rigid imposition of the ancient creeds and confessions or by drawing up a detailed new statement of belief. As with worship, so with matters of belief, the right answers can only be found after unit-

[1] *The Church: Its Nature, Function and Ordering*, pp. 48–52 and 83.

22

ing. This is more obvious today than it was in the long years of negotiation before the inauguration of the Church of South India and, as
will be seen in a later chapter, the issue is by no means closed. But it is
true that responsible Christian leaders everywhere are becoming aware
both of the value and of the limitations of creeds and confessions, however venerable, and that agreement is possible where even fifty years
ago it would have seemed unthinkable. The realization of the inescapable Westernness of all our inherited documents, as seen from
Asia, and of the almost complete unintelligibility of the confessions
apart from Western historical events, has helped to bring this about.
The movement of thought which found expression in the C.S.I. Basis
of Union has attained a much wider recognition, as was shown in the
resolution of the First British Faith and Order Conference at Nottingham in 1964: "While we affirm standards of belief to be an essential
element in the life of the Church, our remaining differences concerning
the use of these standards, and concerning the relation between Scripture and Tradition, though important, are not sufficient to stand as
barriers to unity. They do not separate us at the point of the central
affirmation of our faith, and they can be better explored within a united
Church."[1] It is however, necessary to point out that, had Lutherans
been present in force, this affirmation might have been more seriously
questioned.

Finally, though again this is not universally accepted, to seek unity
effectively, it is vital for all the Churches concerned to be ready to
commit themselves. It is useless to look for unity and, at the same time,
to try to keep open a way back. The loyalty of every member of the
united Church, under God, must be to the united Church and not to
that Church to which he previously belonged. The rules by which he
is bound are the rules of the Church to which he belongs after union,
not those of his past. There is at this point, as elsewhere, a close parallel
with marriage. Just as there can be no such thing as trial marriage because it lacks the essential element of total committal, so there is no
such thing as partial or trial union. The uniting Churches must, from
the beginning, be seeking God's way to their disappearance as separate
entities entirely and forever, or they will never find true unity. That,
in part, is why neither "federal union" nor "intercommunion" can be
held satisfactory, because they do not take seriously enough the denial
of the reconciling work of God in Christ which is inseparable from our
clinging to our distinct identities as Churches. Perhaps only those who

[1] *Nottingham*, p. 75.

have had to undergo the experience of moving back from life in even a limited unity into their previous denominations can fully appreciate how great has been the release from denominationalism and how burdensome is the return to it.

There have been and, no doubt, will again be attempts either by denominations in the West or by groups within them to impose upon those negotiating for unity a rigidity in one or more of these matters which would make unity unattainable. There may be those who want to bind the united Church more tightly in matters of doctrine, worship or discipline than the realities of their own denomination warrant. Yet it remains true that the experience of the Church of South India and the general pattern of those plans of Union which offer any promise of results do, in general, establish these six points as valid. It rests with those who reject some or all of them to produce evidence, by an advance towards unity in some concrete situation, that union is possible without their acceptance.

# III

## PRECONDITIONS OF ANY USEFUL NEGOTIATION

THE TITLE of this chapter must not be understood to mean that any one of the negotiating Churches is right in insisting on prior acceptance of certain demands before it is ready to negotiate at all. Far from it. Such an attitude makes any real advance impossible. That this is true has gradually become apparent and the course of the South India negotiations has definitely helped to make this clear. In the original appeal from the Tranquebar Conference of 1919, there were words which might be taken to involve something of this insistence that there were points on which the members of the different Churches present were not prepared for any compromise. What was said was: "In seeking union, the Anglican members present stand for the one ultimate principle of the *Historic Episcopate*. They ask for the 'acceptance of the fact of episcopacy and not any theory as to its character'. The South India United Church members believe it is 'a necessary condition that the episcopate should reassume a constitutional form' on the primitive, simple, apostolic model. While the Anglicans ask for the Historic Episcopate, the members of the South India United Church also make one condition of union, namely the recognition of *spiritual equality*, of the universal priesthood of all believers, and of the rights of the laity to their full expression in the Church."[1]

At that date something of the kind was probably inevitable. But, in fact, it was unnecessary and unsound in principle. Churches which are prepared to negotiate must already have come to know enough about one another to be sure of two things—that they will meet as Christians and that everyone is ready to consider what anyone else wishes to bring before them. To refuse to discuss unless certain points are withdrawn from that exposure to free consideration, in the light of all the available evidence and of the experience of all Christians, in the presence of the Holy Spirit, is to make real advance impossible. While the Church, in any sense in which men use that word, cannot divest itself

[1] Sundkler, p. 102.

of a real responsibility for holding and proclaiming the gospel in all its truth, it still remains God's truth, not ours, and God must be trusted to look after it. The fear that Christians too often manifest is dangerously near a mistrust of the Holy Spirit.

If we meet to seek Church unity, we meet in Christ. We meet in the context of being His disciples for whom He prays that they may be one, as He and the Father are one, that the world may believe that the Father has sent Him. If not, we are not concerned with the only unity which matters for us as Christians. We meet as those to whom He has given the Holy Spirit. We meet as all within the new creation, all under the new covenant, not merely sinners but forgiven sinners.

The ultimate ground of our unity, as of our being Christians, is, according to the New Testament, the act of God and not any belief of ours or pattern of our behaviour. All the great decisive words at the opening of the Pauline letters are words of God's act, not men's: words like "called", "chosen", "holy", "purchased". The change in the sense of "holy" or "saints" from the divine setting apart to the human attainment of sanctity has gravely obscured the truth of the gospel. If we meet as Christians, we meet with the only equality that matters, as objects of that grace of God which we can do nothing to merit and which we can only accept in faith. On that ground, and on that ground alone, we come to seek together God's way to the better manifestation of that unity which we already have, as His gift, in Christ through the Holy Spirit. On that ground the Churches which send their negotiators must look upon one another as corporately in the one Lord of the Church.

This does not mean that members of one Church (using that word in our modern, if unscriptural, sense) may not be sincerely convinced that their corporate life and teaching express more adequately than do those of other Churches the will of our common Lord. It does not mean that they will not do all in their power to explain and commend to others what they believe that God has shown to them. It does not mean that they will not start with strongly held opinions on the inadequacy of other systems of church organization or of other ways of stating the truth of the gospel. It does mean that they will come trusting God to protect and commend that truth which is His truth and therefore not afraid to examine again in fellowship what they hold most precious. It does mean that they recognize that the members of the other Churches are as genuine in their desire to know and to obey God's will as they are themselves. It does carry with it the humility which conceives that they themselves may be mistaken. Neither sanctity nor sense is the monopoly of any one Church.

This expressed itself in South India from the start of the negotiations in the full recognition that all those who had been baptized within any one of the negotiating Churches must be accepted as baptized into Christ, that all communicants must be received as communicants and that no minister can rightly be required, as a condition of entering into the united Church, to deny either in word or in act the truth of God's calling and grace-gifts for the ministry of God's word and God's sacraments in God's Church. "Wherever Jesus Christ is, there is the Catholic Church."[1] He is not partly present here and more completely present there. It is irrelevant for men to argue, as we too often do, that by our rules He ought not to have been present here, ought not to have worked through this ordinance or listened to this prayer. God is not denominational and it is useless to wish that He were. We knew that the whole Christ had come, through all His divided and imperfect denominational instruments, to take for Himself a people in South India, and we recognized the same Christ wherever He had so come, one Redeemer behind all the differences of expression of belief, patterns of worship, forms of church organization and types of church architecture. Compared to the basic change, within a broadly Hindu society, which Christ makes, denominational variations are marginal. In this respect, Asia and Africa are far nearer to the New Testament situation than is our Western world, and because of that fact the essential unity of all Christians, over against everyone else, is the more plain.

Secondly, it must be recognized that there will never be unity if we try to insist on the acceptance by the negotiating Churches of one particular judgment on those events in the past which led to the separations that we now seek to let God overcome. It is impossible to retrace our steps to the point of disunion. History is not reversible. All the time we have all been within the one Body of Christ and God has been guiding us, in spite of our various disobediences and blindnesses. While it is true that the separations ought not to have happened, it is also true that none of them have cut the resultant denominational bodies wholly away from the Holy Spirit. It is not less important that renewed historical study has made it plain, at least to most scholars, that there is no major separation in which all the right is on one side and all the wrong on the other. We can never know enough about

[1] Ignatius, *Smyrnaeans*, VIII.

past events and the motives of those immediately involved to pass absolute judgments. The Churches which negotiate are where they are because, in spite of all fallible and foolish human beings, God has led them to the point of negotiation with their fellow Christians.

Today we can all admit that even our most cherished leaders in the past had their limitations and that they were themselves only partly free to act in opposition to the mass of their supporters, often less intelligent and less spiritual than themselves. We have become more aware of the power of the organization over the individual and of the total sociological setting of what may seem at first sight to be purely religious disputes. We know that even the greatest reformer is far closer to the traditionalist of his own day than he can be to us. It is useless for one age to sit in judgment on another and to demand that everyone accepts one verdict on the men and the events of the past. There is a sense in which most Church history is unedifying. It is important to understand better than those fed on little party manuals have ever done the real issues that were involved in the events which led up to the Council of Chalcedon and its aftermath of separation, in the breach between Rome and Constantinople, in the history of the Reformation in Western Europe, in the Methodist movement in England and in every major separation among Christians. It is not important that everyone today should agree in their evaluation of those events. This is the more true because, almost everywhere, doctrinal disputes have become so involved with the misuse of power, social and other pressures on minorities by the majority body, injustice and persecution, that a purely theological judgment is impossible. There are few if any Christian Churches which, however enthusiastic about toleration when they were weak, have practised it when they were strong. No Church must be expected to condemn its own past or its own fathers as a condition of union in the present. That will carry with it a readiness to cease from insisting on the condemnation of the past of those other Churches which, by its willingness to negotiate, it recognizes as "in Christ". God cannot build unity on anathemas.

Thirdly, it must be grasped that negotiating Churches are essentially different from big businesses trying to bring about a merger. The Church in all its expressions exists, not for itself, but for God's purposes towards the world. It must finally be controlled, not by its leaders or its members, but by God, unless it is to become apostate. Unity is at bottom a matter of the Holy Spirit. It depends not upon a nice balancing of conflicting interests, an adjustment of organization which will

provide posts for the holders of power in the existing separate structures, a creating of better machinery for the same kind of people to do
the same kind of things with more advantage to themselves and their
fellow members, but upon a leading of men and women by God into
a deeper understanding of the gospel and a heightened awareness of
His power. It is not, fundamentally, dependent either upon human
cleverness or upon human learning, but upon God's grace accepted by
faith. It is an act of God's creative love, within the context of that new
creation in Christ which is and must remain foolishness to the world.
If the Church can be described adequately within merely historical or
sociological terms, there is no redemption.

# IV

## WHAT IS THE CHURCH?

OUT OF THE experience of seeking unity, and still more from life in unity, there ought to come a deeper understanding of what the Church is in the purpose of God. It would be untrue to claim that any one clearly articulated formulation of the nature of the Church underlies the *Basis of Union* and the *Constitution of the Church of South India*. These, it must be stressed, are themselves the results of negotiation by three not yet united Churches. Nor, since the inauguration, has C.S.I. committed itself to any formal definition of the Church. Yet, if we examine the course of the negotiations as they are recorded in Dr. Sundkler's study; as we look at the answers of C.S.I. to the questions addressed to it by the Lambeth Conference of 1948 and by the Joint Committees of the Convocations of Canterbury and York in 1950; as we follow the *Theological Conversations* between C.S.I. and the five Lutheran Churches in South India; something distinctive begins to appear.

By being the Church somewhat more effectively, C.S.I. is discovering a more adequate understanding of what the Church is. It is being shown more clearly what it exists to do, and is therefore challenged to examine its ways of action and its machinery no less than its teaching. Something of this discovery has become available for all Christians, but those who have lived and worked within the fellowship of the Church of South India have inevitably become more aware of it. Effective thinking is closely bound up with responsible decision and action. In 1950, in preparation for the Faith and Order volume on the Nature of the Church, we said: "Many problems of the conference hall that seemed almost insoluble when we faced each other from outside, with an obligation to defend the separate denominational emphasis, have taken on a very different appearance when we find ourselves handling them, as practical issues, within the fellowship of one Church."[1] That has proved increasingly true. In our Conversations with the Lutherans,

[1] *The Nature of the Church*, ed. Flew, S.C.M. Press, London, 1952, p. 227.

the latter more than once commented on the fact that the C.S.I. representatives found no difficulty in agreeing about what they wanted to say, while they, with a common Lutheran inheritance but separately organized and with different national backgrounds, were not always able easily to produce an agreed statement. C.S.I. is a much more united body than I found the Church of India, Burma and Ceylon during my five years as an Anglican bishop. It is far more united than the Church of England.

First, there is the renewed awareness of the Holy Spirit. The Church is a reality in the realm of the Spirit. That does not mean that it is wholly out of contact with the everyday world in which men live and work. It does mean that it has a quality of its own by which it is distinguished from all other patterns of human community. This is a point where the gospel is particularly relevant to India, where communal strife is a tragic reality and where the group or community can too easily be a divisive influence within the national life. The community, in this sense, concentrates the attention of its members on their own advantages and privileges, to the neglect of that concern for those outside these narrow limits which is vital to the well-being of the whole nation. Experience shows how it is possible for the Church in such situations to become, in great measure, a self-regarding community like the communities around it. An example is the ancient Syrian Church in South-West India, which for many centuries ceased to exhibit any desire to draw others into the fellowship of the gospel and accepted the typically Hindu caste pattern in relation to interdining and intermarriage. Both before and after Independence, though the general attitude of Christian leaders has been against any seeking of privileges or safeguards for Christians as a separate group, there have been Christians who would have welcomed an organization not unlike the old Moslem League, aiming at reservation of posts under the Government and other advantages confined to members of what they look upon as the Christian community. If so, the Church would be looked upon as a "pressure group" for the benefit of its own adherents.

This is, inevitably, a particular temptation for a small and underprivileged body in a society where the general pattern is one of communities acting in the interests of their own members. The Church, the community of the Holy Spirit, is called to be different. It is meant to be outward looking, aiming not at getting for its own members but at giving to all. It exists not for itself but for the world. As an outstanding

Indian Christian, Father Paul Verghese of the Syrian Orthodox Church in Kerala, put it to the Nottingham Faith and Order Conference 1964, the Church is not to be like "sheep in the sheepfold with their noses together, keeping themselves warm with each other's breath while their tails keep wiggling".[1] In a country torn by racialism the Church must bear relevant witness by transcending race; in a country divided into competing communities it is vital that it demonstrates the truth of its claim that in Christ all walls of partition are broken down. If not, why should those outside believe in the new creation in Christ?

The truth as God has revealed it in Jesus Christ is that God is love. Therefore at the heart of the Church is love—for God, for those within the fellowship and for the world. This is an intensely practical thing. It must show itself in the actual contacts of daily life, with that down-to-earth realism which marks the first Epistle of St. John. Historically, both in the New Testament and through all history, this love is first apparent in the local group of Christians, men and women living close to one another and in the contact of their work. Its power must be seen in the day to day relations of the members of the Church one to another. The local Christian fellowship IS the Church. It is the point at which the Church meets both the individual Christian and the world. "The Church in any place IS the local Church in the sense that there the Holy Spirit creates a localized community, the Church of God which is in that place. It is NOT the local Church in any sense of being less truly the Church than some organized body of Christians within a larger area. More especially, it is not the local Church in the sense that it derives its existence and authority as the Church by delegation from or through any wider organization or that its relation to its Lord is a mediated rather than a direct presence. The Lord of the Church is there and therefore His Church is there. He is not partly there and therefore His Church is not partly there, or there by derivation from some wider organization."[2]

That statement comes from within C.S.I. It may be compared with two other statements. The first carries the authority of the Legal Board of the Church Assembly of the Church of England. It runs: "The only essential unit of ecclesiastical organization is the diocese, just as the only essential officer is the bishop who presides over it. All spiritual authority in the diocese comes from him, and he has a cure of souls over the whole diocese, although he delegates a share of it by

[1] *Nottingham*, pp. 25 f.
[2] *The Mission of the Local Church*, Hollis, N.C.C. (*India*) *Review*, April 1959.

institution or licence."[1] The second comes from the Fourth World Conference on Faith and Order held at Montreal: "In our discussions of the relation of the churches to the Church we have found it helpful to think not in terms of the churches as parts of the one Church but rather of the Church as the Body of Christ, including the saints of all ages and the Christians in all places, which is both present in, and one with, the local congregation gathered for the hearing of the Word and the celebration of the Lord's Supper according to Christ's ordinance. 'Wherever Jesus Christ is, there is the Catholic Church.' Thus each church or congregation participating in Christ is related to others not by participation in some higher structure or organization but rather by an identity of existence in Christ. In this sense each congregation gathered for the proclamation of the Word and the celebration of the Eucharist is a manifestation of the whole Catholic Church in the very process of becoming what she is in service and witness to the world."[2]

Statements in accordance with the Montreal way of thinking appear in the Plans for Union for Ceylon, North India/Pakistan and Nigeria and, if nothing very explicit on this subject is to be found in the Basis of Union put out for Ghana, that may be because none of the negotiating Churches there were Congregationalist in tradition. The Anglican mythology expressed in the former quotation has been criticized by responsible scholars from within the Church of England, on historical no less than on theological grounds.[3] It is to be hoped that both in England and throughout the Anglican Communion it may soon be authoritatively abandoned. It belongs to that whole way of thinking, bound up with one of the most serious defects of Anglican understanding of the nature of the Church, by which, at any rate within the Church of England, it is possible for a person to be baptized, be confirmed and regularly to receive communion without at any point being explicitly accepted by any specific congregation as a member and without accepting the concrete obligations and privileges of that membership in a local expression of the fellowship of the Holy Spirit.

But the Church is not present and active only at the local level, for it is concerned with the total activity of God in His reconciling of the world. Where God is at work, He looks for and needs an appropriate instrument; and His normal instrument is His Church. As God works at different levels and over areas large or small, so He needs the appro-

[1] *Year Book of the Church of England*, 1965/66, p. 371.
[2] *Montreal*, pp. 45 f. and 81.
[3] *Liturgy and Worship*, ed. Lowther Clarke, S.P.C.K., London, 1932, pp. 714 f.

priate expression of the One, Holy, Catholic and Apostolic Church through which to work. In the world of today, there are many things which cannot be done locally. There are regional, national or world-wide needs which God wants to meet. Sheer Independency is today inadequate and inefficient, once it is realized that the Church, at every level, exists for the sake of the world within the context of God's reconciling act in Christ. What matters is that, at every level, the life of the Church is a life in the Holy Spirit, and that, in the Spirit, Christians discover, through prayer and consultation, what God wants to be done and how He wants them to do it.

This must express itself in a real responsibility of the local Church for things that belong to it, of the diocese for matters at that level, for the whole Church regional or ecumenical, so far as organized action is possible at this time, for what it must do. It will show itself in the way business is conducted. The refusal of the Synod of C.S.I., from its first meeting, to decide any question of importance by majority voting was, in the first instance, justified by the actualities of a Church in which 50 per cent of its membership came from Anglicanism. It ensured that minorities were set free from any fear that they would be overridden by a built-in majority from another tradition. This released us all to seek in common the will of God for us in our immediate situation. But it embodies something of much greater importance, theologically, pastorally and evangelistically. It takes seriously the presence and guidance of the Holy Spirit, through whom it is possible for Christians to come to one mind. The conduct of Church Councils and Assemblies is not always edifying; yet they ought to be plain evidence to unbelievers that those who meet have been redeemed and meet in the Holy Spirit. There is something disquieting in the idea of Christian gatherings which feel it necessary to exclude strangers.

The West, using this term to include North America and Australasia, finds it hard to understand this because of that identification of citizen and Christian which it has inherited from the days of the Christian Empire. For centuries there was no obvious "world" in the New Testament sense, out of which the Christian had been delivered by Christ and for the sake of which he had been called and set apart within the Church. There was no dominant alternative pattern of living, with its roots in a religion other than Christianity. The Christian of New Testament days was as manifestly eccentric as is the Christian in India now, but as the Christian in our Western world still does not feel himself to be. Something of that older situation has recurred behind the Iron Curtain. There, too, no one can drift into being a Christian. Christianity is not the line of least resistance and the Church does not exist by inertia. This fact helps to explain why so many of the Plans for unity have been produced in Asia and Africa, where Rome never ruled and where the dominant culture patterns owe little to Hebrew, Greek or Latin. Where everyone is baptized—all or almost all in infancy—it is difficult to see baptism as that decisive act of God which it is in the New Testament. For the light and darkness, life and death, of the Pauline Epistles, men tend to substitute the drabness of varying shades of grey. C.S.I. did not discover the truth of mission as the context within which the Church exists, or of the Holy Spirit as the decisive mark of both Church and Christian, but it gave them expression. It has learnt more about them in the course of its life and it has helped others to grasp them and to try to express them in their own setting and in terms of their own obedience to the one Lord.

# V

## THE FAITH OF THE CHURCH

THE PHRASE "Faith and Order" is well known and the movement so
described holds an important place in the developing ecumenicity now
expressed in the World Council of Churches. Yet it is worth reminding
ourselves that it is a form of speech more natural to those within the
English tradition than to others. *Foi et Constitution* may be the recognized equivalent in French but it does not in fact carry the same over-
tones and undertones, and I remember at Montreal a Spanish-speaking
delegate from South America, a Lutheran, saying that there was nothing in Spanish that gave the same meaning. It goes back in England
at least to the Savoy Declaration of 1658, where the Independents thus
stated their position: "That amongst all Christian States and Churches
there ought to be vouchsafed a forebearance and mutual indulgence
unto Saints of all persuasions, that keep unto, and hold fast the necessary foundations of faith and holiness, in all matters extrafundamental,
whether of Faith or Order."[1] It thus springs from a time when the
assumption that every citizen must worship God within the fold of one
Church organization had in England broken down; when the attempt
to substitute a Presbyterian uniformity for the uniformity of the episcopally ordered Church of England had manifestly failed; and when
the common enemy, if it may be so described, was a restored Stuart
monarchy with a restored Anglicanism as its concomitant. It is, in a
good sense, a phrase of realistic expediency, not an absolute distinction.

It was, during the negotiations which led up to the inauguration of
C.S.I., generally accepted that all concerned were agreed on matters of
Faith and that the difficulties were mainly in the sphere of Order. This
reflects the backgrounds of the negotiating Churches. The great
majority came from Anglicanism or Methodism, both in their English
forms. Neither tradition has ever possessed any fully articulated body

---

[1] Quoted in *Documents of the Christian Church*, ed. Bettenson, 2nd ed. O.U.P.,
London, 1963, p. 353.

of distinctive doctrines. Curiously enough, the Reformed tradition, as it appeared in South India, has played an unexpectedly small part in the theological education of the Indian ministry. The majority of the members of the South Indian United Church were linked with Congregationalism, whether through the London Missionary Society or the American Board of Commissioners for Foreign Missions, and shared the general Independent hesitation about the imposition of credal statements as conditions of Christian fellowship. Nor were the early negotiations carried on at a time favourable to theological seriousness. It was largely taken for granted that all three negotiating Churches held the essentials of the Christian faith. Suspicion that the united Church would lack safeguards against heresy, and that among its ministers and members there were some who were far from orthodoxy, came almost entirely from outside and, in many cases, from those who disliked the whole trend of the negotiations and disapproved of the pattern of the united Church which was going to appear if they succeeded. Heresy is always a good stick with which to beat a dog to which you have already given a bad name.

Much of this was, in reality, irrelevant to the actual situation of the negotiating Churches. They were all bodies which drew the mass of their adherents from the villages. Few Christians were highly educated and, in some areas, a large proportion were illiterate. They were surrounded, not by a sophisticated humanism, but by the superstitions of rural Hinduism. As the C.S.I. said in 1950 in its reply to Lambeth: "We think it right to draw attention to the fact that our position as a small Church in the midst of a vast non-Christian population, which we are seeking to win for Christ, delivers us from some kinds of temptation to theological inadequacy which are apt to attack Churches more securely placed."[1]

The situation has changed even since 1947. Education is spreading and more Christians have moved into the towns. The old unquestioning acceptance of the Bible finds itself challenged in India as elsewhere by what are set forth as the proved truths of modern science. The more Christians are drawn into the main stream of national life, the more they find themselves asking the same questions which men and women everywhere are asking, and the less relevant some of the old answers appear to be. It is useless to blame the *Basis of Union* and the *Constitution*, as put out in their final form by the Joint Committee in 1941, for trying to meet the needs of that time and for seeing things as the men

[1] *Church of South India*, Church Information Board, London, 1950, p. 33.

of that date saw them. What they said cannot be lifted out of its date and context in South India and transferred unaltered to a plan for union elsewhere and in this present day. But the experience of the negotiators in South India may have valuable lessons for those who are seeking unity now.

The original approach, as Dr. Sundkler shows, was deeply influenced by Bishop Palmer. He wanted to get behind the divisions that had arisen in and after the fifth century. In matters of belief he was insistent that all attempts to go beyond the Nicene Creed had brought only disunity. This is summed up in the statement in the pre-1929 *Basis of Union* that the uniting Churches accept the Apostles' and Nicene Creeds as witnesses to the faith and as "containing a sufficient statement thereof for a basis of union". The same point was made in the words at the opening of the Section on the Faith of the Church: "The uniting Churches hold the Faith which the Church has ever held in Jesus Christ." The Holy Scriptures were referred to as "the ultimate standard of the faith".

Within the negotiating Churches this formulation came under criticism from two sides. There were those from the S.I.U.C. who were suspicious of any credal statement, whether as an illegitimate hindrance to the free and honest expression of contemporary individual belief in the context of the needs and questions of the India of their own day, or as tending to substitute for a living personal commitment to Jesus Christ as Saviour the more or less formal acceptance of an intellectual statement. It has to be remembered that these were the times which saw in the West the rise of that so-called Liberalism or Modernism which found its expression in such things as the Girton Conference of the Modern Churchmen's Union in 1921 or, with a certain time-lag, in the report of the Laymen's Commission sent out from U.S.A. entitled *Rethinking Missions*. The extremer claims made on behalf of individual subjectivity were checked within the South India United Church by its experience in having to suspend from the ministry an able pastor on the grounds of the Christological inadequacy of his teaching. Yet, that the two concerns of the critics had a real validity was explicitly recognized by the insertion in the *Basis of Union* of a note: "The uniting Churches accept the fundamental truths embodied in the Creeds named above (sc. Apostles' and Nicene) as providing a sufficient basis of union; but do not intend thereby to demand the assent of individuals to every word or phrase in them, or to exclude reasonable liberty of interpretation, or to assert that those Creeds are a complete expression of the Christian faith."[1] With this should be taken the paragraph in Chapter V of the *Constitution*, on the Ordained Ministry of the Church, which says: "The Church of South India here declares that no acceptance of a written standard is sufficient for this (sc. ordination) or for any of the purposes for which such standards are used unless there be also an inward and personal experience of union with God in Christ."[2]

The other and later attack upon the original formulation was due to the influence of Karl Barth, mediated through the missionaries of the Basel Mission working within the Malabar Church Council of the S.I.U.C. Their concern was not to make things easier for the "Liberals" but to ensure that there was due acceptance of "the Holy Scripture of the Old and New Testaments as containing all things necessary to salvation and as the *supreme and decisive* standard of faith".[3] They were also concerned to make it plain that there had been in the history of the Church falling away and real reformation in the understanding and statement of the faith and that history must be taken seriously. There cannot, in fact, ever be a return to a time before questions were asked, once they have been asked. The separation between East and West, the Reformation, the movement associated with the name of John Wesley—all these and other events are part of the total reality with which we today have to reckon in our seeking to be loyal to the full gospel.

There is little evidence that critics from the Anglican side have given much serious consideration to the explanations which C.S.I. has put out. In spite of the statement in the 1950 report of the Joint Committees of the Convocations of Canterbury and York: "After considering the Answer to our first question we are fully satisfied as to the credal orthodoxy of the Church of South India,"[4] the older form still appears in the Ceylon Scheme practically unchanged. It has to be remembered that Anglican preponderance among the negotiating Churches in Ceylon is very great, that Anglo-Catholic influence is strong, and that a guarantee had been given at an early stage of the negotiations that the Anglicans would not accept any Scheme which involved a breach of full communion with Canterbury. North India/Pakistan has gone further, as has Nigeria, but both keep the phrase

[1] *BU*, p. 72.
[2] *C*, p. 33.
[3] *C*, p. 4. *BU*, p. 71. Italics mine.
[4] *Church of South India 1950*, p. 9. Cf. *Lambeth 1958*, ii, p. 47.

"the Faith which the Church has ever held".[1] Ghana, as generally, shows most evidence of thinking for themselves.

Looking back, it is difficult not to feel that much of this argument was in fact more the expression of emotion than of reason. While the C.S.I. assertion that "the phrase 'the faith which the Church has ever held' contains so many ambiguities that it would require elaborate definition to make it serviceable for the purpose of a Constitution" is true, the same comment might be made about the expression which is used in the C.S.I. reply, "the historic faith of the Church",[2] which appears to have reassured the Joint Committees. There is, in fact, no escape from the problem. Every human formulation is in the terms of the thinking of a particular age and society. It employs certain dated categories and asks its questions in those forms which are within its own inheritance and relevant to its own needs. There can be no automatic and impersonal guarantees of the orthodoxy either of a Church or of an individual. The Quaker, Stephen Grellet, visited Geneva in 1813 and found, as his biographer writes, that "Geneva had sadly fallen from its ancestral faith, and proved how vain are historic names, orthodox creeds, and Scriptural formularies when the Spirit ceases to animate the lifeless form. The clergy at that time were, with scarcely an exception, Socinian."[3] In the face of a widespread questioning of traditional formulations of the Faith, some valued the original expression as a kind of reassuring incantation, just as others clung to an insistence on the authority of Scriptures. Both, rightly interpreted, were and are true, but both need to be interpreted, and that really takes us all back to the starting point. What happened within the Negotiating Committee before the Inauguration of C.S.I. and what has been said and done afterwards have had their part in the gradual realization that all the Churches have a common problem. This may be seen in the Montreal report *Scripture, Tradition and Traditions*.[4] We are all asking new questions and all, in varying degrees of clarity, asking the same questions. We shall do better to ask them together.

It is worth emphasizing the growing realization that the intelligible and relevant confessing of Christ to the world of Asia or Africa must be done by the Christians of those areas and in terms of that common conceptual and linguistic inheritance which they share with their non-

[1] cf. *Lambeth 1958*, i, p. 33.
[2] *Church of South India 1950*, p. 32; Bell, *Documents 1948–1957*, p. 21.
[3] *Memoirs of Stephen Grellet*, ed. Seebohm, London, 1860, I, p. 267.
[4] *Montreal*, pp. 50 ff.

Christian fellow citizens. In a right sense there must develop an indigenous theology, which is only just beginning to appear. It is important not to bind the Asian and African Churches too tightly in the swaddling bands of Western theological thinking and expression. It is also true that practical considerations help to set us free from some of the traditional patterns of controversy. When members of C.S.I., of the Lutheran Churches in South India, and of the Baptists, met in 1949, we soon agreed that in fact we all had certain patterns of instruction which were used for the preparation of candidates for baptism, where we were dealing with those capable of a personal act of faith, or for confirmation where we practised it; that this was needed both by the generality of instructors, who were often not highly educated, and by those under instruction, some at least of whom were illiterate, and that the Churches all found themselves setting out these formulations with a measure of authority and approval. Our meeting resulted in an *Agreed Statement* entitled *The relation of doctrinal and confessional statements to the being of the Church*[1] which deserves more general consideration than it appears to have received. I suspect that it would have been impossible to have reached such an agreement had there not been first the negotiations over so many years, and then the life in the one Church of South India since 1947, which made us able to approach both Lutherans and Baptists with a new confidence and freedom.

At the point at which negotiations have become real, there will be no doubt, on the part of those Churches immediately concerned, that all are fully Christian at the deepest level, even if there be still a desire for more adequate formulations to be agreed upon. The criticisms of what is said will, at that point, come mainly, if not entirely, from outside. Some of them will be of value and will call attention to obscurities or to the need to reconsider proposed wordings in the light of the experience of the Church elsewhere. Others will be of little relevance, because they will either reflect the controversies and fears of the Church that makes them, rather than show any deep understanding of the actual situation of the negotiating Churches, or will be little more than rationalizations of resistance to any union which will involve radical challenge to the traditional ecclesiastical set-up in the country of the critics. Christian obedience is obedience by particular people in particular circumstances. It is always possible that they will be mistaken in their decisions. If those outside try to decide for them and to *impose* their decision on them, they will almost inevitably be wrong.

[1] *Agreed Statements*, pp. 9–11.

This raises the whole question of the relationship between Churches, in the sense of organized autonomous units and, more particularly, between Churches in the West and those elsewhere, where there is still a large element of financial dependence. Because of past history the younger Churches are organized and equipped with institutions on a scale which has little relation to their own economic resources. A breaking of fellowship will inevitably involve serious financial dislocation and real hardship for many individuals. That a Church might so betray the truth of the gospel, whether in doctrinal aberration or in conduct, that a breach became inevitable, few would deny. Yet it is important to remind ourselves of the complexity of the issue.

The following quotation from a statement drawn up by a Swedish Lutheran, an Indian Baptist and myself from C.S.I. for a joint consultation is relevant. In particular, what is said in the second paragraph about legal or social penalties, which had individuals in mind, would apply no less to financial penalties which fell upon a whole Church as a consequence of a breaking off of fellowship.

"The question of the unit of authority needs to be further considered. Logically, it may not be obvious why the Church (in the sense of the local Congregation) should be allowed authority over the individual believer while a group of Churches is allowed no such authority over a local Church. But, with equal logic, the independence of Dioceses, or of Provinces, or of National Churches might be questioned. We are none of us, for reasons of Scripture and history, prepared to accept Papacy. Failing that, the problem of authority residing in a number of independent units remains.

We need to examine further whether "coercive" authority is, at any level, compatible with Christian principles. The New Testament does show a real authority being exercised, in the way of exclusion from the Christian fellowship. In later times, and in some places now, this is accompanied by legal disabilities or social boycott. This is far more open to question.

It is essential to remember that the One Universal Church can never act by constitutional methods, for only a small part of it is at any moment here on earth. However large and representative a Council, it only represents, in the natural sense of the word, the Christians now alive. Only if those present are in fact guided by the Holy Spirit will their decisions be His decisions and, in the true sense, decisions of the Church. There are no external guarantees that this will be or has been the case. The decisions of the great Ecumenical Councils won acceptance gradually in the judgment of the living Church."[1]

Christian confidence is confidence in the God who does not desert us even in our mistakes.

[1] *More Conversations between Lutherans, Baptists and the C.S.I.*, C.L.S., Madras, 1949, pp. 24 f.

# VI

# THE WORSHIP OF THE CHURCH

THE CONSTITUTION of the Church of South India, as has been already noted, allows great freedom in the pattern of its worship, and places the responsibility for the ordering of the worship of every congregation on that congregation with its minister.[1] In the stage of negotiations this was, for some, a concession to the demands of those of another tradition rather than any recognition that it was in itself desirable or right, but later experience in unity has related this to that deeper understanding of the nature of the Church, which has been discussed in Chapter IV. It must be admitted that by no means all congregations are alive to the creative possibilities of their responsibility. It is worth noting that the C.S.I. Constitution explicitly provides safeguards against that ministerial autocracy in the matter of changes in the forms of public worship which has brought about bitterness and division.[2]

Further, there are provisions which, though seldom used since the coming into existence of C.S.I., might be required. A congregation might, in its worship, diverge so far from what can be looked upon as Christian, or might employ forms and patterns so inadequate as expressions of the wholeness of the gospel, that some check is needed. This is dealt with by allowing the bishop "in the case of grave irregularities in public worship to forbid their continuance and any such prohibition shall remain in force pending any action which the Executive Committee of the Synod of the Church may take thereon".[3] This has never had to be done but, in other parts of India, difficult situations have arisen which have called for a real "testing of the spirits". Where there is a desire for change there may often be a minority which objects, and neither are all ministers wise, nor all lay people reasonable. Here again the bishop can act, but it is clear that he acts not as a judge but as a father in God, seeking to bring about mutual understanding in love rather than to impose a solution.

One important element in the life in union ought to be the mutual

[1] C, pp. 8 and 49 ff.      [2] C, p. 52.      [3] C, p. 22.

enrichment which comes from the sharing of previously separate traditions of worship and the more adequate meeting of new needs and new opportunities, as they arise. Here both the Diocesan and the Synod Liturgy Committees are playing a valuable part, in making possible creative experiment and co-ordinating the lessons which come from their employment. It is impossible for a committee to devise a satisfactory form of service which can be given final authority before it has been well used. But, no less, the ordinary congregation is unlikely to know enough about the general principles of liturgy, and about the total riches of the whole Christian inheritance to be able to provide the most adequate pattern of worship. There must be a real measure of guidance and advice. The Synod Liturgy Committee has already an impressive record of achievement. But it needs to be stressed that none of the services which it has drawn up and which have received the approval of the Synod is compulsory for any congregation. Diocesan and Synod services, which are obviously not wholly within any one previous denominational tradition but express the new unity, stand on a different footing. In particular the Ordinal, which is concerned with acts of the Church of South India in its corporate capacity, is used at all ordinations and consecrations.

The general impression given by the *Basis of Union* and the *Constitution of the Church of South India* is one of concern to safeguard all members from any imposed change in the ways of worship to which they were accustomed. This is understandable. As has been already pointed out, Anglicans formed the major body among the negotiators, and Anglicanism was and is associated, in the minds of many outside and inside, with the Book of Common Prayer and with the Act of Uniformity. Even when that Act does not apply, there is still powerful the ideal of one form of worship to be found in every church, and that has spread even to those countries where much of the worship of Anglicans is in another language. In India, it was only with much searchings of heart, and in the face of considerable doubts on the part of ecclesiastical lawyers, that even minor divergencies from the most literal translation of the 1662 Prayer Book were permitted. The Tamil still suffers from strange transliterations of Septuagesima and its following Sundays. It was essential to make sure that after union the ex-Anglicans would not use their majority to impose upon the whole Church the Prayer Book or some modification of it. The provisions are, in general, backward looking, although there is a statement that it is desired to conserve for the united Church all the riches of the separate inheritances.[1] Even that would have been, in one sense, possible within an imposed uniformity. The same general pattern has been taken over into North India/Pakistan, Ceylon, and Nigeria.

This backward look is a little disappointing, for one of the un-expected but most welcome fruits of unity in South India has been the release of creative thinking in this sphere of worship. What has come out of union is not only a mutual enrichment by the sharing of what already existed in separation but something fresh. The most successful service forms which have come from the Synod Liturgy Committee are just those where the scissors-and-paste combination of something from the Anglicans, something from the Methodists, something from the Congregationalists and something from the Reformed, with a glance at the Syrians, has been abandoned in favour of a bold attempt to express the best available insights of the whole Christian tradition of worship in the context of South India today.

The point at which the realization of the Church as being the whole body of Christians shows itself is in the more active part given to the congregation in the new C.S.I. Services. This is perhaps most notice-able in the Lord's Supper. No one who has used both the 1662 Book of Common Prayer form and the C.S.I. Liturgy can fail to be aware of this. But it is seen also in the positive share given to the congregation in Baptism and in Confirmation. The prayers are not just the prayers of the minister but of the whole Church in its local manifestation. The acts are the acts of God in answer to the prayers of His people there gathered. The congregation, both at Baptism and at Confirmation, solemnly accepts those baptized or confirmed and pledges itself to fellowship with them in Christ. The same emphasis upon the whole Church, not just the bishop, as actively concerned, is seen in the Services of the C.S.I. Ordinal.

Yet there is recognition in the North India/Pakistan and Nigerian plans that the united Church ought to develop forms of worship more expressive of the particular inheritance of those so drawn into unity. The Ghana plan is more explicit. "The united Church will . . . seek to develop forms of worship in which the distinctive gifts which God has given to the people of Ghana may be reverently used and offered."[2] This may be compared with the more general statement in the C.S.I. Constitution: "The Church of South India desires . . . conserving all that is of value in its Indian heritage, to express under Indian conditions

[1] C, p. 11.
[2] Proposed Basis of Union, Ghana, 1963, p. 21.

and in Indian forms the spirit, the thought and the life of the Church Universal."[1] Indigenization is now recognized to be important. So much of the worship of Christians in Asia and Africa is terribly foreign, reflecting only too faithfully the background of the early missionaries, whatever their nationality and denomination may have been. In many places there are to be found not the patterns of today, even within the denominational tradition of the founding Church, but those of the late nineteenth or early twentieth century, untouched by the creative developments which have had so much influence in the West. Much Christian worship in Asia and Africa is sterile rather than creative. For example, in South India the ex-Anglicans in particular have shown unwillingness to use the C.S.I. Service of the Lord's Supper and some of the visitors there from the Church of England have found themselves urging the value of that rite and pointing out its superiority to the form of the 1662 Book of Common Prayer. The process of fruitful study, consultation and experiment is beginning and it is helped on by the fact of unity, which both brings people into close contact with one another and does something to set them free from the enslaving power of custom. But indigenization is not something which can be imposed on unwilling nationals by enthusiastic foreigners, and some of what has been done is unhappily artificial.

Here the Liturgical Movement has much to contribute, and the call of Montreal for thinking, studying and experimenting together was echoed by the British Faith and Order Conference at Nottingham.[2] This is also closely linked with a reconsideration of the kind of buildings which are used and the arrangement and furnishing, which can too often carry to the worshippers lessons which are very different from what is meant by the new forms of service and from the intention of preacher and teacher. The loosening of denominational ties which goes with the coming into existence of a united Church can help to promote all this re-examination. It can also encourage those not yet united to see what can be done in the way of enrichment and provide forms, already tried, for their own experimental use. In something of the same way, though this can only be an interim arrangement, the fact that there are C.S.I. forms, which are wider than those of any denomination and which have won widespread praise, gives, to those planning for union, services which can be used in the beginning of life together, until their own development allows them to produce what

[1] *C*, p. 3.
[2] *Montreal*, pp. 69 ff., *Nottingham*, p. 76.

they need for themselves. In South India, there were no such forms ready and it was the sense of need to express at the Lord's Table, not our past disunity, but our life together, that led the C.S.I. to produce the Service of the Lord's Supper.

One important example of the creative effect of C.S.I. is to be seen in the radical change in the attitude of Anglicans towards the Book of Common Prayer. In the past it has been taken for granted that the possession of Prayer Books which, with whatever local variations, plainly all derive from the same roots, was one of the things which held the Anglican Communion together. Even in 1948, the Committee of the Lambeth Conference which reported on the Anglican Communion could say: "This essentially Anglican authority is reflected in our adherence to episcopacy as the source and centre of our order, and the Book of Common Prayer as the standard of our worship."[1] The report of the Lambeth Conference held in 1958 shows a very different approach, recognizing that there must be far-reaching developments and a much wider element of variety, if worship is to be adequate.[2] There is also the production of a Liturgy for Africa which is by no means a modification of the basic pattern of 1662 but an attempt to produce something which is true to the totality of Christian experience and relevant to the needs of Africa today. That this is deeply influenced by what has been done in South India is plain to anyone who examines the proposed service. The point is made clear by Archbishop Brown, who was himself both the Secretary of the Committee of the Lambeth Conference of 1958 which considered the Book of Common Prayer and also, at the request of the Archbishops of the Anglican Communion in that area, the compiler of the Liturgy for Africa. In *Relevant Liturgy*[3] he prints both this form and the C.S.I. Order of the Lord's Supper, and discusses the influence of the latter, of which he himself, while still a presbyter of the Church of South India, was the principal architect.

What is vital is that there be a wider exchange of information, both about creative studies in worship and about the new developments elsewhere, together with opportunities for members of one Church to join, over a sufficient period of time, with other Christians who worship differently; but it must be long enough to allow of the initial sense of unwelcome strangeness to be in a measure overcome. A united

[1] *Lambeth 1948*, p. 86 (part ii), quoting *Lambeth 1920*.
[2] *Lambeth 1958*, ii, pp. 78 ff.
[3] *Relevant Liturgy*, L. W. Brown, S.P.C.K., London, 1965.

Church offers great opportunities for this, but it needs to be done on a wider scale and as a preliminary to union, and demands a searching reconsideration of inherited ways and regulations, in the light of our realization of our fundamental unity in Christ, which we must seek to allow him to manifest more effectively.

# VII

# THE MINISTRY IN THE CHURCH OF SOUTH INDIA

THE STARTING POINT for any profitable consideration of the C.S.I. handling of the ministry and of the criticisms of it must be an accurate understanding of what has actually been done and is being done there. The Scheme of Union deliberately concentrated its attention on what the various ministers of C.S.I. are going to do. It does not try to produce any comprehensive doctrine of the ministry or to answer theoretical questions. The *Basis of Union* and the *Constitution* allowed the Church to get going. Many questions were left to be answered, if they must be answered, by the united Church in the light of its own experience of life in union.

Thus the *Constitution* stated what the bishop, the presbyter and the deacon will do, within the total life of the Church. It deliberately avoided certain traditional terms; it refused to answer certain questions posed in these terms. This has continued within C.S.I. For example, it does not use the title "priest" but prefers "presbyter". This is intelligible enough in terms of the West. It was even more natural in the South India of the negotiations, where the gap between the Roman Catholic and other forms of Christianity was at times so wide that popular non-Christian speech could refer to them as two distinct religions. Nor was there enough awareness of modern thinking within the Roman Church itself in a good deal of the presentation of the doctrine of the Mass and, with that, of the priesthood. Further, in a setting where animal sacrifices had not yet ceased and where offerings to various deities were frequent in the villages, where the majority of the Christians lived, the desire to distinguish the Christian minister from the sacrificer is not surprising. In fact I know of no Indian language in which Christians—Roman, Syrian or other—use for their ministers the same word which Hindus would apply to their priests.

Similarly, there is a refusal to say that there are three "orders" in the ministry, there is an avoidance of the expression "character", and it is not insisted that there must always be a passing through the stages of the ministry, though it is stated among the rules, that bishops must be chosen from those who are already presbyters. It is important for Anglicans, especially those of the "Catholic" tradition, to realize more than they often do, that their kind of language is not the only way in which it is possible to speak about the Christian ministry.[1] The categories which they are accustomed to employ are, very largely, conditioned by the West. The traditional structure is deeply coloured by the administrative pattern of the Roman Empire, particularly in its later and more bureaucratic form. So far as purely Latin developments are concerned, these are expressed in terms of, and influenced by, that Scholastic philosophy which is neither universal nor inevitable. It is most important to leave to the developing Churches of Asia and Africa the greatest possible freedom to discover their own answers to their own questions, to develop their own ways of expressing the truth of the gospel in their own ordered life, in terms which are meaningful to them and through patterns which correspond to their own traditions and their own setting. Exported terms and categories, together with foreign structures, can exercise a sterilizing effect on those to whom they are deeply alien. This is the greater danger where, as is still too generally true today, most advanced theological study or examination of the history of the Church can only be done in the West, in languages which are not that of the student, and in a total society very strange to that within which his Church must live and witness. Even where there is a real mastery of a European language, as there often is to a degree which puts many Westerners to shame, there can remain depths which are accessible only to the mother tongue and which are untouched by anything learnt in what remains more the speech of the head than of the heart. As has been said, one can live in a foreign language but one cannot die in it.

The same kind of terminology is found in other Plans, though, once again, Ceylon goes further in the direction of trying to satisfy Anglicans by stating: "It is the intention of this Church to continue and reverently to use and esteem the three-fold ministry of Bishop, Presbyter and Deacon which existed in the undivided Church." This might seem to be irreconcilable with that "parity of ministers" to which great importance was attached by some of the negotiators in South India. Yet it has to be recognized that the great discrepancies in power, salary and position between the Indian minister and the foreign missionary made it difficult for Indians to attach any very clear meaning

[1] *Nottingham*, p. 51.

to this important phrase, nor does it fit easily into the context of what is still a highly stratified society.

The aim of the Church of South India was well stated in 1953 by its Theological Commission, commenting on the Ceylon negotiations, in which one of its dioceses, that of Jaffna in North Ceylon, was and is involved. "No Scheme of Union can succeed unless it is plain that what is aimed at is a genuine continuance, within the wider fellowship, of the whole inheritance of the separate ministries mutually enriched, and not the extinction of non-episcopal ministries in order that they may be replaced by an episcopal ministry which itself remains essentially what it was before."[1] This needs to be remembered when considering services for the Unification or Reconciliation of now separate ministries.

The original Tranquebar message had spoken of bishops in the historic succession exercising their ministry constitutionally. The fact of episcopacy was what was held to matter, "not any theory as to its character". It has subsequently become clear that this really seeks to exclude the imposition of any *one* theory rather than to suggest that no one is to have any interpretation of what it means. There was and still is a desire to safeguard the members of the united Church from finding themselves compelled, in the interests of a view held by one section of Anglicans, together with the great majority of Christians Eastern and Western, to accept a theory of episcopacy which would involve the condemnation of their own denominational past. But already, experience within C.S.I. shows that an understanding of episcopacy, which is not the precise repetition of what has been held before and elsewhere but is positive and forward looking, does develop within unity as it could not do either through theoretical study of the past or from negotiations between separate Churches, some of which have no bishops.

It is unnecessary here to recapitulate the course of the negotiations out of which the *Basis of Union* and the *Constitution* came, for they are set out in Dr. Sundkler's book. What is important is to grasp the resultant pattern, for that is often misunderstood. The starting point is that no Church exists invertebrate. It has from the beginning a ministry, within its life and necessary for its life. To ask which comes first, Church or ministry, is unprofitable. They cannot exist apart. The negotiating Churches recognized one another as Churches. They sought God's way to become one Church. They knew that any true

[1] Synod *Minutes, 1954,* p. 147.

union must, at the deepest level, be the result not of human negotiations, however necessary they might be to clear the way, but of an act of God. They believed that, when He unites Churches, He unites them entirely, with their ministries. It was therefore right that at the Inauguration a representative of each of the uniting Churches not only read the resolution of the Governing Body of his Church and placed on the communion table a signed copy of the *Basis of Union* and the *Constitution*, but also, at the same time, laid there a book containing the signed statement of all the ministers of his Church "declaring their assent to the *Basis of Union* and their acceptance of the *Constitution of the Church of South India*". Church and ministry are offered to God, for His acceptance and for His creative act. Then came a prayer, with this petition: "In obedience to Thy will and led by Thy Spirit, as we accept one another as fellow members and fellow ministers, do Thou strengthen the bonds between us and unite us and make us one body, Thyself, O Christ, being its Head." It was after this that the Bishop presiding declared that the three Churches "are become one Church of South India and that those bishops, presbyters, deacons and probationers who have assented to the *Basis of Union* and accepted the *Constitution of the Church of South India* and whose names are laid upon this holy table, are bishops, presbyters and deacons in this Church."

It is still often said that C.S.I. has not got a unified ministry. In the frequently misunderstood provision about what will happen at the end of thirty years are the words "a fully unified ministry within the Church", and this can be linked with what is said in the earlier section about "Unity in Ministry and Life within the Church of South India".[1] This recognizes that the inauguration of the Church of South India "has initiated a process of growing together" and that one element in complete unity is that "all members of the Church should be willing and able to receive communion equally in all its churches".[2] C.S.I. has a ministry which others, particularly Anglicans, divide into two groups, those who have been ordained by bishops and those who have not. Within C.S.I. there are still those, from the Anglican tradition, who regard it as wrong for them to receive communion from ministers not episcopally ordained. No other of the parent Churches makes this distinction. Even the Convocations of Canterbury and York in 1950 agreed that members of the Church of England, when in South India, "may accept the hospitality of the Church for the performance of

[1] *C*, p. 18. *BU*, p. 84.
[2] *C*, p. 12. *BU*, p. 85.

priestly functions or the receiving of holy communion" without any insistence that the minister must have been episcopally ordained. Yet it is clear that, in this sense, the ministry is not yet fully unified. A distinction can be drawn by those who wish to draw it.

Within C.S.I. itself the unwillingness of some ex-Anglican congregations to accept a minister not episcopally ordained, whether as a permanent arrangement or on a special occasion, may be no more than a general objection to all change, closely linked with a refusal to use the C.S.I. Order of the Lord's Supper or to agree to any alteration of the forms of service to which they have grown accustomed. There can, at times, be equal unwillingness to accept a minister from another tradition, even when he has been episcopally ordained within C.S.I. The theological arguments are often not good theology. Yet the undertaking not to impose on any congregation a ministry or form of service to which there is conscientious objection is pastorally right and, in my experience, has been applied even where the claim that the objection is conscientious is extremely shaky. Not all critics in England or elsewhere have been well-advised in their readiness to accept stories of oppression, whether the oppressed were supposed to be suffering for "Catholic principles" or for "Independency". This is not to say that, in what too easily degenerated into factional quarrels running back into a distant past, everyone on any side has always behaved entirely Christianly. Bishop Partridge, who was himself Anglican bishop in Nandyal, has some illuminating things to say about that particular dispute, which could be paralleled elsewhere.[1]

"The Pledge", as it was called, is an expression of that love without which neither orthodoxy of belief nor correctitude of order is of any value. But the recognition that love must determine all our handling of this sort of question does not alter the fundamental basis of the Union, which was accepted by the Governing Bodies of all the three Churches concerned. That meant: for the Anglican, the General Council of the Church of India, Burma and Ceylon; for the South India United Church, its General Assembly; and, for the Methodists, the Methodist Conference in England, with which rested the constitutional responsibility for the final decision. In the *Basis of Union* it is stated: "Wherever union takes place, it comes into being only by the working of the spirit of Christ, Who is both truth and love. In His spirit of love all the ministers of the uniting Churches will from the inauguration of the union be recognized as *equally ministers of the united Church*

[1] *The Way in India*, W. A. Partridge, S.P.G., London, 1962, pp. 66, 69 f.

*without distinction or difference.*"[1] That could hardly be plainer. It is in complete accord with this provision that the five bishops of the Church of India, Burma and Ceylon then working in South India and hoping to work within the Church of South India when it came into existence issued the following statement in 1946: "All who have the status of Presbyters in the United Church are capable of performing all the functions assigned to Presbyters in the United Church by the Constitution of that Church in every congregation of that Church . . .no Presbyter of the United Church will exercise his ministry in a congregation where members conscientiously object to his ministrations." They also made their own position clear by saying: "After the inauguration of Union we, as Bishops of the Church of South India, shall be ready ourselves to receive communion at the hands of any Bishop or Presbyter of the United Church."[2]

Obviously, as was stated in the preamble to the Resolution by which the General Council of 1945 finally adopted the Scheme of Union in South India, the C.I.B.C. itself, as a Province of the Anglican Communion, continued to be bound by its Constitution and Canons;[3] but it did then as a Church officially accept the Scheme, the *Basis of Union* as well as the *Constitution*, in order that the four Anglican dioceses in South India might be free to enter into union with the South India United Church and the Methodists. It is irresponsible to speak as if this were not the constitutional act of the Province. It is equally irresponsible to suggest that the 96 representatives who made up the General Council on that occasion were not aware of what the Scheme contained, after so many years of vigorous and at times intense discussion and controversy. I remember at the General Council in 1945, when I was responsible for proposing the resolution on this matter, making the point very clear and, at the next General Council in 1947 when the question about the Pledge and its interpretation was under discussion, I challenged any who disapproved of what the five Southern bishops had said to disown us officially and explicitly by resolution of the General Council; but nothing was done.

So far as the Church of South India is concerned, its ministry is one, and it has acted on that conviction, with pastoral consideration for those not yet freed from past ways of thinking, but without admitting

---

[1] *BU*, p. 69. Italics mine.
[2] Sundkler, p. 321. Full text in *Church Union in South India*, A. J. Arangaden, Basel Mission Press, Mangalore 1947, pp. 183 f.
[3] Sundkler, p. 334.

any essential incapacity or inferiority in any of its ministers, however ordained. The difficulty is an Anglican one and, because the law of the land is involved through the Act of Uniformity of 1661 and the Colonial Clergy Act of 1874, in a special sense one that concerns the Church of England. Anglicans, together with some ex-Anglicans in C.S.I., may think that the Church of South India has two grades of presbyters. There are some among the ministers of C.S.I. who feel unhappy about the fact that, out of pastoral consideration for the consciences of certain members of the Church, they cannot be sent to exercise their ministry everywhere without limitation. Yet it remains true that the Church of South India has its own position clearly stated in this phrase of the *Basis of Union*, in its *Constitution* and, after twelve years of life as one Church, in the *Agreed Statement* on *The Church and the Ministry* which came out of the Theological Conversations with the Lutherans.[1] The Church of South India has come to value episcopacy highly, but does not look upon episcopacy or, in particular, tactual succession back to the apostles, as essential to the existence either of the Church or of the Ministry.

The same principles have governed the receiving into its ministry of those ordained outside it. The *Constitution* lays down that, for the space of thirty years, "the ministers of any Church whose missions have founded the originally separate parts of the Church of South India shall be received as ministers of that Church, if they are willing to give the same assent to the Governing Principles of the Church and the same promise to accept the Constitution of the Church as shall be required from persons to be ordained or employed for the first time in the Church".[2] Very rapidly it became necessary to decide how to deal with ministers from other than the actual founding Churches, and it was decided that C.S.I. would accept, on these conditions, any minister from any Church whose ministers would have been accepted by any one of the three Churches involved in the union. In effect, any minister ordained by what can be regarded as a responsible Christian Church, whether it be episcopally ordered with or without the succession, or not, may be accepted to minister in C.S.I., if he is otherwise satisfactorily qualified for the post in question.

Again, because of a question which actually arose, the original requirement of the *Constitution* that anyone to be consecrated as a bishop must be "already a presbyter" has been clarified. A new clause,

[1] *Agreed Statements*, pp. 20–4.
[2] *C*, p. 17.

in the revised Rules for the Election of a Bishop, reads: "No person shall be nominated unless he is a Bishop or a Presbyter of the Church of South India, or a Minister of equivalent standing in a Church with which the Church of South India is in fellowship."[1] This makes plain that, in this vital matter of eligibility for nomination as a possible bishop, the Church of South India looks upon all its presbyters as on precisely the same footing, and also that it accepts the ministers of any Church with which it is in fellowship, however that Church itself be ordered.

The "intention and expectation of the Church of South India" is still "that eventually every minister exercising a permanent ministry in it will be an episcopally ordained minister."[2] But how and when that will come about it is impossible to forecast. In the words of the reply to the Lambeth question on this matter: "We are united in one Church; our parent Churches are divided. If it is now insisted that we state what our permanent relation with them is to be, we can only say that we can be content with nothing except that they should be united as we are. So long as they remain divided our position must remain anomalous from the point of view of any one of the divided Churches. But from the point of view of the historic faith of the Church we must surely judge that the real anomaly, the scandal, is that the Church should be divided. We have promised at the end of 30 years to give equal weight to two principles: that our own ministry shall be one and that we shall maintain and extend full communion with our parent Churches. As things stand, these two principles are irreconcilable. They can only be reconciled when the parent Churches now divided are united. Our act of union is an act of faith in the Holy Spirit that He will bring this about. We cannot therefore say more than the Constitution has said about what our successors will do in circumstances which we pray may be profoundly different from those in which we now are."[3]

[1] *Synod Minutes 1958*, p. 106.
[2] C, p. 17.
[3] *Church of South India, 1950*, pp. 37 f. Bell, *Documents 1948–1957*, p. 35.

# VIII

## THE UNIFICATION OF THE MINISTRY

THERE WAS very heavy pressure on the Church of India, Burma and Ceylon and, in particular, on those Anglicans in South India who would go out from the Anglican Communion to become part of the Church of South India, to postpone any final decision and action until after the Lambeth Conference had met in 1948. But rightly, as I am more than ever convinced, the Inauguration took place on September 27, 1947, and the Conference at its meeting in the following year had to give advice to the Churches of the Anglican Communion on their attitude towards the Church of South India and, in the light of its existence, towards other plans for united Churches in which Anglicans were or might be concerned. Both the Committee on the Unity of the Church and the whole Conference thanked God for the measure of unity locally achieved. There are expressions of warm encouragement and hope. There is a very reasonable refusal to pass final judgment on something as new as the Church of South India then was. Yet, as too often with Anglicans, the generous and forward looking verbal expressions are not adequately matched by actions. The basic effect of the Conference so far as Anglicans everywhere are concerned is to say that in the sphere of the ministry the South India methods of dealing with the transition from disunity to unity must never be repeated. "The unification of the ministry in a form satisfactory to all the bodies concerned, either at the inauguration of the union or as soon as possible thereafter, is likely to be a prerequisite to success in all future proposals for the reunion of the Churches."[1]

It is true that this is no more than advice and that every Province is free to accept or reject it; but this is by no means the whole truth. Not only is there the great weight which naturally attaches to a resolution of the Lambeth Conference. The Anglican Churches in Asia and Africa are still heavily dependent upon help from outside, and in particular, from the Church of England, both for men and women and

[1] *Lambeth 1948*, p. 40 (part i).

for money. Opportunities for further study and experience are highly valued. As a consequence of their entry into the Church of South India, even though this was done with the constitutional approval of the Anglican Province of which they had formed part, the Anglicans in South India were deprived of the endowments of two dioceses held in England and of some £10,000 annually which they had been receiving from certain missionary organizations in that country. One major Missionary Society appeared to assume that all its missionaries in South India would also wish to withdraw. In fact, almost all stayed on and it proved possible to support them from other sources. There has been a modification of this attitude but the whole of the support lost has still not been made good. It is not to be wondered at if advice, with these hard facts behind it, tends to be taken as something more than advice. Western-based institutions—and the Anglican Communion is in essence a Western-based institution—have still a long way to go before they grasp the full implications of their past and present paternalism in relation to the growth of the Church in other parts of the world. Asian and African Christians are generally too polite to say just what they feel about it. Some of them are too deeply implicated in the advantages of the system to speak frankly. Others trying to express the truth do so with a violence which makes it only too easy to discount their valid criticisms as mere emotional nationalism. Anyhow, since 1948 every Plan in which Anglicans are involved has envisaged, as a vital part of the inauguration of the united Church, some form of unification of the ministry by a laying on of hands by ministers, at least one of whom is a bishop within the historic succession. It is in this way hoped that there will be from the first full intercommunion between the united Church and the Churches of the Anglican Communion.

There is little evidence that the method of South India would not be acceptable to other Churches currently engaged in union negotiations anywhere. The problem is an Anglican problem. The 1948 Lambeth Conference asked for more theological study about the Church and the ministry,[1] stated that "the integral connexion between the Church and the ministry should be safeguarded in all proposals for the achievement of intercommunion through the creation of a mutually recognized ministry" and, in the matter of "Supplemental Ordination", called for further consideration and study by theologians.[2] If this has taken

[1] *Lambeth 1948*, p. 20 (part i).
[2] *Lambeth 1948*, pp. 64–6 (part i).

place, it has not come to light, and the impression has been given that "unification of ministries" is the Anglican "line", and that it is safer to go that way in order to gain recognition by, and support from within, the Anglican Communion. The other Churches have agreed to what they do not themselves particularly like or want, with the hope that in this way Anglicans may be willing to enter into union. It is noteworthy that, for a number of years, the plans for union in Nigeria were going ahead along the South India way, and that the Churches concerned invited the then Moderator of the Church of South India, Bishop Sumitra, to visit them. One of the questions which was put to him was about the ministry, and he answered it with great care. Then the Lambeth Conference of 1958 strongly recommended that the Ceylon scheme be taken as a model "since only so does it seem likely that the desired result (sc. full communion with the Churches of the Anglican Communion from the outset) will be achieved".[1] A change was then made. It is difficult to believe that theological arguments alone brought the Anglicans in West Africa to urge this change of policy or the other Churches there to agree to it. A method which has resulted in real and growing unity in South India has been abandoned in favour of another which has yet to work anywhere and which, so far as the Ceylon Scheme is concerned, has failed, in spite of the Lambeth commendation, to lead to that promise of full communion from the Church of England which was one of the main objects of its adoption.

The position might well be clearer if it were based on a theological conviction shared by all Anglicans. In fact, this notoriously is not so. The Anglican Province concerned agreed to the plan proposed for the Church of South India. Half the Church came from Anglicanism and the experience of eighteen years of life in union has not made them wish that they had remained in their previous separation. The *Conversations between the Church of England and the Methodist Church* make the issue very plain. "It is well known that widely differing interpretations of episcopacy and priesthood exist side by side within the Church of England. Some Anglicans regard episcopacy as one possible form of church government, desirable it may be, but not essential; others regard episcopacy as an essential constituent of the Church, a necessary strand in apostolic continuity. Some Anglicans place the emphasis in the interpretation of priesthood upon its sacrificial and absolving functions, in the daily offering of the Eucharist and in re-

[1] *Lambeth 1958*, i, p. 38. Cf. *Unity in Nigeria*: Garrett and Jeffery, E.H.P., London, 1965, pp. 34 ff.

gular sacramental confession; others hold views of the ministry differing in no essential way from those prevailing in non-episcopal communions. This diversity is based on the co-existence within the Anglican tradition of elements which point now in one direction and now in another and may be differently emphasized. The full extent of such liberty of interpretation is only possible within the strictest invariability of episcopal ordination. For, while it is possible to hold a 'low' view of episcopacy and priesthood within a strict invariability of practice, it becomes impossible to hold a 'high' view where this invariability is broken. It is therefore reasonable that the Church of England, while agreeing to the Methodist requirement of liberty of interpretation, shall itself ask for assurance that episcopal ordination will be strictly invariable within the Methodist Church after relations of full communion have been established."[1]

The difference of conviction is there stated without concealment. What is not recognized is that theological issues are not permanently avoidable, even if they may be left unsettled for many years. There come times in the course of history or, if we like so to phrase it, in the providence of God, when a Church may find itself faced with an inescapable decision, because it is necessary to act one way or the other. To try to avoid decision or to postpone it is in reality to decide in favour of the conviction which makes action illegitimate. In the early years of the Church's life it was not necessary to settle whether or not a Christian Jew might eat with a Gentile who had put his faith in the gospel. Plainly, many among the first Christians were convinced that incorporation into the old Covenant people of Israel by circumcision was "an essential constituent of the Church". Peter's experience at Caesarea, the preaching to Greeks at Antioch, and Barnabas' approval, and, above all, the work of Paul and Barnabas, made it clear that God did not confine His grace within those limits. It could have been argued that, while it was permissible for Paul to believe that circumcision was not essential, yet the continuance within the Church of those who held the opposite belief was only possible if there were the strictest insistence in practice on circumcision and that therefore this must be invariable. At the least, there must be separation between Jewish and Gentile Christians at the Lord's table. But it is plain that freedom of opinion with the strictest invariability of practice was here something which Paul absolutely refused to countenance. He acted in

[1] *Conversations*, Church Information Office and Epworth Press, London, 1963, p. 48.

accordance with his conviction and tried to bring all other Christians to see how vital was the issue. Once the question had been asked in the context of action, there could be no way of escape from facing it and giving an answer.

The Theological Commission of the Church of South India put this very clearly in 1953. "The negotiating Churches (sc. in Ceylon) cannot by any formula escape the necessity of answering the question whether, when e.g. in the Church of Scotland a man is ordained to the Ministry of Word and Sacraments in Christ's Church by laying on of hands with prayer, he is so ordained or not."[1] It is not enough to give a merely verbal answer. Experience over the years has shown that it is impossible to devise any form of words which those skilled in ecclesiastical diplomacy cannot evacuate of their apparently plain meaning. It is only necessary to refer to the statement presented in 1923 on behalf of the Church of England representatives to representatives of the Free Churches: "It seems to us to be in accordance with the Lambeth Appeal to say, as we are prepared to say, that the ministries which we had in view in this memorandum, ministries which imply a sincere intention to preach Christ's Word and to administer the Sacraments as Christ has ordained, and to which authority has been solemnly given by the Church concerned, are real ministries of Christ's Word and Sacrament in the Universal Church."[2] The only decisive form of reply is action. When the five South Indian bishops said, in 1946, "after the inauguration of Union we, as Bishops of the Church of South India shall be ready ourselves to receive communion at the hands of any Bishop or Presbyter of the United Church", they left no loophole for misunderstanding because they said what they were going to do. Real questions are always particular questions, in particular circumstances and at definite points of time. They are answered by a decision to act one way or another and a refusal to act is itself a decision and an act.

Between 1930 and 1948 much had happened, and there were clearly a number of the Bishops at Lambeth in 1948 who were shaken at the prospect of the disappearance of the Anglican Communion, within not many years, from considerable areas of Asia and Africa. It is also true that there has been, and has continued to be a hardening of the general Anglican attitude to members of other Churches, especially in the matter of Holy Communion. While previously, in what may be

[1] *Synod Minutes 1954*, p. 146.
[2] *Documents on Christian Unity: A Selection 1920–1930*, G. K. A. Bell, O.U.P., 1955, p. 55.

called a missionary situation, where Christians were few and where members of one Church might be cut off by distance for long periods from the worship of their own denomination, there had generally been a great measure of freedom, this has tended in many places to decrease. Even if non-Anglicans are still welcomed to communion by Anglicans, there has come to be more desire to provide Anglican ministrations, perhaps very infrequent, for scattered Anglicans in places where there are already congregations of Christians of another tradition. With this goes a tendency to suggest to those Anglicans that, even if they worship with their fellow Christians, they should not join with them at their Communion services or, at least, not to the point of communicating with them. This is not true everywhere, but I have found it in a number of different parts of the world. One effect of the Ecumenical Movement on Anglicans as on others has been a revival of denominational consciousness, apparent both in the theological and in the organizational spheres.

The aim of those in the other Churches who have agreed to this kind of "unification of the ministry" is a laudable one—to make it possible for Anglicans to enter into a united Church without previous abandonment of any conscientiously held belief. It obviously calls for a similar readiness on the part of Anglicans not to ask for any denial of the beliefs of others as a precondition of unity. Otherwise we are back once again at absorption rather than union. No one ought to be expected either to condemn his own fathers in the faith or to deny the work of God within that part of the Christian Church through which he has been brought to the knowledge of God in Christ and within which he has received the Holy Spirit. It is hoped that unification may be effected by a service of laying on of hands with prayer, in which God is asked to give whatever He sees to be needed for the fulness of ministry in the united Church. With this goes a carefully drafted statement that no denial or questioning of any prior ordination is involved. In some Plans the meaningless statement that this rite is not "reordination", appears, a phrase which ought to be banished, along with "rebaptism", from all ecumenical discussions. It is nowhere said that the rite is or is not ordination. Those from Churches not episcopally ordered would refuse to agree that it is ordination, for that would deny that they had already been ordained; while some Anglicans would remain wholly unsatisfied if it were unambiguously stated that it is not ordination, for only ordination by a bishop in the historic succession can give them that security which they desire. Yet it must not be defined as ordination for all, for they themselves will not question their own orders.

This openness of understanding is central to all the plans which have been put forward, and with it goes the insistence that the rite proposed is essentially one without precedent. That is of the greatest importance. There cannot be precedents for that healing of divisions which has never yet taken place. Human nature being what it is, there will always be those who wish to persuade themselves or others that what is being done is really the same as something done in the past and that there is no genuinely new step; but they are wrong. It is not necessary, however, for there to be any over-nice inquiry into the way in which individuals convince themselves that they are justified in taking part in this kind of service or into the ideas which they individually may hold about what God is giving and doing, whether to the ministers from their own tradition or to those of the other Churches. What is far more doubtful is whether any one of the uniting Churches can properly lay down the sense in which it, as a Church, understands the rite, either as bestowing episcopal ordination upon those not previously so ordained or, in natural reaction to such an insistence, as being in no sense ordination at all.

That the united Church will not itself be committed to the belief that episcopal ordination is essential to the existence of Church or ministry is, in all the Schemes and Plans, unmistakable. They all, in words borrowed from or equivalent to those in the *Basis of Union* and the *Constitution of the Church of South India*, state that "the fact that other Churches do not follow the rule of episcopal ordination shall not in itself preclude the united Church from holding relations of communion and fellowship with them".[1] This in itself may seem to some to make any acceptance of such plans impossible. Clearly, for those who believe that God has laid down one pattern of Church Order as His will, for all times and all places, any compromise on this point is intolerable. Only since modern scholarship has shaken the older denominational certainties have useful discussions become possible. For if man's salvation is bound up with acceptance of a body of revealed truth, and if within that truth is a particular pattern of the Church's ordering, then no one has any right either to depart from that ordering himself or, by allowing them still to believe that their ordering is approved by God, to countenance the continuance of others in a life contrary to God's will. This is equally true for the convinced Papalist,

[1] *C*, p. 11. *BU*, p. 78.

the Episcopalian, the Presbyterian, or the Independent. He may recognize with thankfulness God's gracious working outside the patterns of His will, but he must not abandon the duty of bearing witness to that divine will. Churches which are not ready to be humble about this whole issue are not yet ready for serious negotiation about unity. But it is necessary to recognize the impossibility of reaching full agreement while the negotiating Churches are still in their separation. The essential aim of any viable plan must be to make it possible for life in unity to begin, leaving many decisions to be taken by the united Church. The act of obedience involved in this submitting to God's will, as we experienced in South India, releases fuller resources of understanding for those who enter into union without any deliberate abandonment of what they hold to be true but with deep awareness that everything will look very different when unity has been brought about.

That there are serious criticisms to be levelled against every form so far produced for this unification of ministries by a special service is true. One thing which has become clear is that the original idea, as put forward by the Lambeth Conference of 1920 in its *Appeal to all Christian People*,[1] that every Church should give authority to the ministers of every other Church by what it considers an appropriate ceremony, which for the Anglicans would mean that bishops would lay hands on all ministers not ordained already by bishops in the historic succession, is unsatisfactory. It implies that each Church, in its separation, possesses certain treasures which it can impart to others, and obscures the truth that the giver of all good things is God, and God alone. So far as the ministry is concerned, it results in what is unquestionably an ordaining of the ministers of non-episcopally ordered Churches, which, however much it may satisfy Anglicans, is totally unacceptable to those other Churches. At the heart of all Plans now under consideration is the offering of the total ministry of the united Church to God, with the prayer that He will accept it and give to every member of it all that is needed for the fulfilment of that ministry in the united Church. It is an act of the united Church, not of the separated Churches, and it is carried out by the ministry of the united Church, which will include both its episcopate and its presbyterate.

Up to this point there is, fundamentally, little which differs from what was done at the inauguration of the Church of South India, though the prayer is more explicit and so is the Statement of Intention which precedes the service. Few, if any, of those seriously concerned

[1] *Documents, 1920–1930*, Bell, p. 1.

about unity would refuse to take part in such a ceremony. The real problem arises because, unlike what was done in South India, the rite includes the laying on of hands. It has been explained that this is a ceremony with more than one meaning, and that its use here does not necessarily involve the belief that some or all of the ministers are being ordained. That is true; but its relevance depends upon the degree of mutual trust and understanding which exists among those concerned. Plainly it will be easier for such a rite to be agreed to where there has been practical recognition of the non-episcopal ministries because Anglicans, and in particular Anglican bishops and priests, have already shown themselves ready to receive communion at the hands of other ministers at united gatherings or when visiting non-Anglican Churches. We were clear in South India in 1947 that any ceremony whatever which might suggest that, in our dealings with the existing ministers, there could be any thought of ordaining those not episcopally ordained must be avoided. It was for this reason that even the suggestion that they be given a copy of the Bible was not accepted, because that is given in the Anglican rite of ordination. It has to be recognized that there was—and still is—a deep suspicion about the straightforwardness of Anglicans, and a feeling that any Scheme which Anglicans as a whole are prepared to accept must, hidden somewhere, include an episcopal ordination and therefore involve a refusal genuinely to accept the ministers of non-episcopal Churches as truly ordained. This is particularly the fact in England, where the privileged position of the Church of England and the social snobbery that has too often gone with it have left deep scars. Perhaps, in the providence of God, the Church of South India has done something, just because it has not received the wholehearted approval of Anglicans, and because its bishops, even if previously Anglican bishops, have not been invited to the Lambeth Conference. It was certainly my experience both in England and in Scotland that the fact that Anglicans in South India had been ready to pay the price of entering into union with non-Anglicans gave me a welcome and freedom of entry among non-Anglicans which would have been unthinkable before 1947.

The trouble is with the laying on of hands. This is of vital importance just because, unless it is included in the service, the hesitations of some will not be alleviated. Without it, while the attitude of the Anglican Communion remains what it is, full communion between the united Church and the Churches of the Anglican Communion will not be possible. So far as the situation in England is concerned, it is hard to believe that any Judge would hold that the requirements of the Preface to the Ordinal or of the Colonial Clergy Act had been met and that a minister had received episcopal ordination, if episcopal hands had never at any point been laid upon him.

Two further criticisms have been made, neither without weight. First, it is pointed out that, if every time union takes place there is to be a similar unification of the ministry, some ministers may have to take part in such ceremonies two or three times in their lives and that this will tend to bring the whole method into question. Those in the West tend to underestimate the possibility of union coming quickly, and fail to realize the importance of keeping any united Church on the move, of preventing it settling down into an inward looking concern which forgets that its union is only a small step towards that union of all Christians which is the aim of all local unions. Yet if, at this point of time, advance is possible in this way, through a service of unification, it may be right to follow it. We must recognize both that we cannot know how the future will develop and also that any resultant united Church, once it has come into existence, is absolutely free to make its own decisions. By constitutional procedure it can alter any provision in its Constitution. The decision about how another and wider union is to come about will be made by it and the other Churches then concerned in the negotiations. When that wider union is inaugurated, all the negotiating Churches, including the united Church about which we may now be thinking, will die in order that God may create something new and nearer to His will.

Secondly, so much attention has been focused on the meeting by the united Church of Anglican demands that it has often escaped notice that the requirements of a service of unification for every minister coming to take up a permanent ministry within the united Church will apply to Anglicans no less than the others. It will mean that there will not be "full communion", as defined by the Lambeth Conference 1958,[1] between the Churches of the Anglican Communion and the united Church, for full communion is there specifically stated to include mutual recognition and acceptance of ministries.

There are bound to be untidinesses in any Plan. What matters is that the final decision be taken by those actually concerned, who have come over the years to know and trust one another in Christ and who will themselves live in union as a result of that decision. Those outside and not directly involved must be willing to accept their decision

[1] *Lambeth 1958*, i, p. 35.

without trying to dictate what it shall be; and, sure that God does not desert us even if we make mistakes, to continue in the closest possible fellowship with the united Church and so to help it to learn more of God's will.

# IX

## ORDINATION

PLAINLY SOME of the difficulties about proposed services for the unification of the ministry spring from differences about what ordination means. In South India there was agreement from all sides that ordination is not to the ministry of a denomination, but to the ministry of the universal Church, and that it is once for all. That is true in the other Schemes and Plans under consideration. It is agreed that ordination is not to be repeated when someone is appointed to a new charge or when, after ceasing to exercise his ministry for a time, he resumes it. There will also appear to be agreement that in the service of ordination there is more than just a recognition by the Church, in whatever sense that word be used, of the divine call. In the words of the C.S.I. *Constitution*: "God . . . in response to the prayers of His Church, and through the words and acts of its representatives, commissions and empowers for the office and work to which they are called the persons whom it has selected."[1]

The older way of thinking was that a man either was ordained or was not ordained, which meant also that either he was acceptable to another Church as a minister, after whatever promises and renunciations might be held necessary in the sphere of belief, or he was treated as a layman. The distinction, inherited by Anglicans from the pre-Reformation pattern of thinking, of "orders" and "jurisdiction" is here useful. Valid orders do not in themselves confer on a man the right to exercise his ministry wherever he chooses. He must be duly sent and appointed. Whatever their phraseology, all organized Christian bodies recognize this necessity. In this sense, all the ministers of a united Church at its inauguration need to receive authority from that united Church to exercise their ministry and to be appointed to specific places or spheres. It is proper that prayer should be offered to God for them, that He will grant them the gifts and graces which they will need for the fulfilment of their ministry within the united Church. By the fact that separate

C, p. 10.

Churches are united into one, the area within which this authorization is effective is extended. They become acceptable to Christians who before would not have received them. So far, no serious problems arise.

But one aim of the proposed rites of unification is that the conscientious convictions of those who believe "that episcopacy is of divine appointment and that episcopal ordination is an essential guarantee of the Sacraments of the Church"[1] may be recognized and any scruples set at rest. Yet it is also a vital part of any such proposed rite that it be used "without prejudice to the reality of the Ordination previously given and received in whatever form".[2] An early way of trying to describe this was to speak of Supplemental Ordination, seeing all ordinations—and all sacraments—in a divided Church as in some measure defective because the actual Church which was God's instrument was not in fact the whole Church but only a part of it. *Lambeth 1948* made some very pertinent criticisms of this way of thinking and they need to be taken seriously.[3] Those who have drawn up the forms to be used in the Schemes now under consideration hope that they have advanced beyond the idea of Supplemental Ordination and that any thought of quantification of orders is avoided. There is point in what was said by the C.S.I. Theological Commission in 1953: "It seems to us that the whole idea that all ministries are defective by reason of our divisions needs far more thorough examination before it can be accepted. The reality of God's gifts is not dependent on the obedience of those who pray for them or upon the measure of their understanding of them." The Commission went on to say: "We do not consider that the divisions of the Church involve any defect in the divine gift in Baptism, though they do grievously hinder our understanding of it and of our life within the fellowship of the baptized. We would suggest that a similar approach with regard to the divine gift in ordination is a truer one."[4] The whole of our Christian life is, or ought to be, a progressive discovery of what we have already received by the grace of God.

A more limited form of this same problem is raised by those who seek to draw a distinction between "ordination" and "episcopal ordination", while asserting that they recognize the reality of that previous

[1] *BU.*, p. 76. Cf. *Lambeth 1948*, p. 50 (part ii).
[2] *Basis of Union, Ghana*, p. 17.
[3] *Lambeth 1948*, pp. 64 ff. (part ii).
[4] *Synod Minutes 1954*, pp. 146 f.

ordination which was not episcopal. An example of this is the resolution of the Church of Wales (Anglican) about entering into full communion with the proposed Church of Lanka (Ceylon). This ran: "We believe that the Church of Wales would enter into full communion with the Church of Lanka providing that the negotiating Churches are agreed that in the service of the unification of the sacred ministry episcopal ordination is bestowed on those not previously so ordained. We think that a statement to this effect is necessary in view of conflicting opinions on the precise significance of the service of unification. We readily acknowledge that the service does not call in question any ordination already received."[1]

*Lambeth 1948* rightly insisted that "The integral connection between the Church and the ministry should be safeguarded in all proposals for the achievement of intercommunion through the creation of a mutually recognized ministry."[2] This applies with no less weight to all attempts to provide a united Church with a unified ministry by a rite of the kind under discussion. In fact, however, Anglicans have an unhappy legacy dating from the unbalanced Tractarian emphasis on the validity of the ministry of the Church of England, treated in dangerous isolation from the Church itself. There is, on the one hand, the refusal to deal firmly with those persons who, while being able to show that they have been consecrated to the episcopate within a tactual succession which goes back to someone who can be recognized as a true bishop of a responsible Christian Church, yet are themselves outside any such Christian fellowship. The most that the Lambeth Conferences have felt able to say about those ordained or consecrated by such "wandering bishops" is that they must be given conditional ordination before they are permitted to exercise any ministry within the Anglican Communion.[3] Anglicans are not ready to say decisively that there can be no ordination outside anything which can be called the Church, even if the "ordainer" can show an unbroken tactual succession. These "bishops, archbishops and patriarchs" present a real problem in India and they have to be dealt with on sound theological principles.

Secondly, there is the idea that a Church which has never had, or has mislaid, the historic episcopate can be given it by the participation of Anglican bishops in its consecrations, previous to and as a precondition of full intercommunion with the Churches of the Anglican Communion. This was the proposal made by the Church of England to the

[1] Quoted in *Church Union News and Views*, November 1962, p. 57.
[2] *Lambeth 1948*, 40 (part i).    [3] *Lambeth 1958*, i, p. 42.

Lutherans on the Continent of Europe, it having been agreed that the Churches concerned "hold the most fundamental doctrines of the Christian faith". It is noteworthy that the Lower House of the Convocation of Canterbury, representing the clergy other than the diocesan bishops, refused to go further than approving the proposal that, if requested to do so by the authorities of the Lutheran Church concerned, the Archbishop of Canterbury might commission a bishop to take part in the consecration of a Lutheran bishop. They did not agree to a Lutheran bishop being allowed to take part in the consecration of a bishop of the Church of England.[1] There is no such difficulty about Swedish bishops, since the Swedes have retained the succession from the bishops of pre-Reformation times. This again is open to serious criticism. If two Churches are not in full fellowship and communion with one another, it is theologically difficult to see how they can properly share in anything so intimately an act of Christ in his Church as the ordaining or consecrating of ministers. The refusal to receive communion at such a service inevitably suggests that the ordination and consecrations of the Church which has not retained this succession are looked upon as invalid or, at the best, too doubtful to be accepted by the Church of England, and that the essential participant is, by Anglicans, looked on as the Anglican bishop. How unfortunate this unbalanced emphasis on a succession of the ministry isolated from succession in the Church is can be seen both by the unwillingness of influential Lutherans to accept any plan for episcopacy within the historic succession, for fear that it will be used to cast doubt upon their existing ministries and, perhaps more strikingly, by the care taken by the Danish Church to see that even where Swedish bishops join in the service of consecration of a Danish bishop they do not lay hands upon him. The matter may be summed up in two phrases which came out of a recent discussion. Ordination must not be seen as a kind of infection. Interconsecration should not be possible without intercommunion.

If this is accepted, then it will be necessary to examine with care certain proposals. In Ceylon the new bishops, at the inauguration of union, will "be consecrated by three duly authorized bishops, if possible from outside Ceylon, representing different Church traditions and acceptable to all the uniting Churches".[2] It is the hope of the Anglicans in Ceylon that the Churches of the Anglican Communion

---

[1] *Documents on Christian Unity*, 3rd series, Bell, O.U.P., London, 1948, pp. 146–57.

[2] Bayne, p. 33.

will already have undertaken to enter into relations of full fellowship with the Church of Lanka, as soon as it comes into existence, but it is not clear whether this is thought of as essential or what other bishops are envisaged. One could come from the Church of South India, which is already involved in that one of its dioceses, Jaffna, is in Ceylon and is taking part in the negotiations. In Ghana, four ministers representing Churches outside Ghana "which will, we hope, have agreed to be in communion with the united Church" will join in laying hands on the four ministers who will officiate at the service of unification.[1]

Something similar is now proposed for North India/Pakistan. Four representatives from Churches outside North India, including two bishops in the historic episcopate, will be associated with the representatives of the seven Churches in the first laying on of hands. On this, Canon Sully, Convenor of the Anglican delegation to the Joint Committee, writes: "This will mean that three bishops in the historic succession will be taking part in the Prayer and the laying on of hands on the three ministers (including a bishop) who become the first nucleus of the united ministry and who carry out the rest of the central act of unification. As in the ancient tradition there should be at least three bishops taking part in a consecration of any new bishop, this addition will emphasize the aim of securing a truly catholic continuity in the ministry of the united Church and particularly of its episcopate, and may help to remove any possible doubts and scruples."[2] The article does not make clear whether this matter of the relationships of the Churches from which these representatives come to the united Church has been given any consideration.

In Australia, the proposals have been drawn up without the participation of the Anglicans, though they are now definitely interested. A majority of the representatives on the Joint Commission, including all the Congregationalists and most of the Presbyterians, but with more hesitation among the Methodists, want to have bishops from the start and urge a concordat with the Church of South India, so that bishops from that Church might take part in the consecration of the Australian bishops. Thereafter there would be close fellowship and consultation, but the two Churches would retain their full autonomy.[3] The comment of the C.S.I. Theological Commission is here pertinent. "Our conception of the integral relation between the ministry and the Church

---

[1] *Basis of Union, Ghana,* pp. 18 f.
[2] Sully, in *Theology,* November 1965, p. 522.
[3] *The Church: its Nature, etc.,* p. 83. Cf. pp. 51–57.

would mean that an order of ministry could only be communicated on the establishment of relations of full intercommunion. This the concordat, if concluded, would establish."[1]

The emphasis in all this discussion tends to be on the Anglicans, because they have in the past refused to accept into their ministry any who have not been episcopally ordained. But there are problems elsewhere, which show that we all need to think more deeply. Even while negotiations were still in progress in South India and there was, from the side of the non-Anglicans, including the Methodists and the Presbyterians, the most determined insistence that there must be no action which even seemed to question their ministry, the Church of Scotland ordained a Methodist minister who had been working in South India and wished to accept a charge in Scotland. Again, while Anglicans have always accepted men ordained within the Roman Church as validly ordained, and one such has worked within the Church of South India, some other Churches of the Reformation have not done so. There will, of course, always be marginal cases where it is impossible to be sure that what was done was done by a responsible body which can in any sense be held to be a manifestation of the Church of God and that it really intended to do what the Church does when it ordains. Already in C.S.I. we have sometimes had to say that we could not accept as satisfactory what purported to be an ordination and must ordain the man in question before we gave him work as a minister. The Church, in any of its expressions, has to rely upon the Holy Spirit and make the best judgment it can, sure that God will not abandon His people if they make mistakes. He is not nearly as pedantic as some experts tend to suggest.

Finally, there is what may be one of the most important insights yet given to the Church of South India. To quote the preface to its *Ordinal*: "An ordination service is the rite by which one of these ministries is conferred. It is an act of God in His Church. 'The Church of South India believes that in all ordinations and consecrations the true Ordainer and Consecrator is God, who, in response to the prayers of His Church, and through the words and acts of its representatives, commissions and empowers for the office and work to which they are called the persons whom it has selected.' (*Constitution* II, 11.)"[2] On this Dr. Ratcliff commented: " 'Who ordains?' The average Anglican, and others in the medieval tradition, would answer, no doubt, that the

[1] *Synod Minutes 1964*, p. 92.
[2] *Book of Common Worship*, O.U.P., London, 1963, p. 160.

ordainer is the bishop." . . . He then quotes the passage which is given above and goes on: "The presiding bishop therefore serves on one side as the agent of God and on the other as the representative of the Church. Here, whether consciously or otherwise, the South Indian authorities have adopted the ancient and, it may be added, the obviously right conception of the matter."[1] This insight was not easily reached. The Lambeth Conference of 1930, though it disliked the participation of presbyters in the consecration of a bishop, was prepared to tolerate it but said: "If adopted, it should be fully explained that the presbyters did not take part as Consecrators."[2] This was wholly unacceptable to many if not all the non-Anglican negotiators and discussion over two days produced no solution. Then, as Dr. Banninga, Secretary of the Joint Committee at the time, told me, "After this long debate all members became silent and bowed their heads in prayer. After several minutes Bishop Loyd rose and said very quietly, 'Would this reading do? It should be understood and taught that the real Consecrator is God.' Immediately all agreed and it was so recorded." Thus nine ministers of C.S.I., three from each tradition, laid hands on the first new bishops, and it is wrong on C.S.I. principles to say that 'the consecrators were the ex-Anglican bishops'.[3]

It stands there, but its consequences have not yet been fully thought out. If the real Consecrator is God, and if He acts in response to the prayers of His Church, then it has to be asked whether anyone can both assert that the non-episcopal Churches are "true parts of the One, Holy, Catholic, and Apostolic Church", to quote *Lambeth 1958*,[4] and at the same time deny that God acts when they pray and ordain a man, in the words of the Ordinal of the Church of Scotland, "to the Office of the Holy Ministry in Thy Church, committing unto him authority to dispense Thy Word and Sacraments, and to bear rule in Thy flock". The new Ordinal of the Church of South India has already attracted considerable attention. It may well help towards a rethinking of the meaning of ordination and to an asking of new questions which will allow Christians, too long bogged down in the well-worn ruts of ancient controversies, to discover the way forward to a fuller understanding—an understanding which does more justice to the wholeness of God's revelation and to God's working in our separate histories than can any of the traditional arguments.

[1] Article in *Theology*, January 1960, p. 8.    [2] Sundkler, pp. 218 and 250.
[3] Buchanan, 'The Church of England and the Church of South India' in *All in Each Place* ed. Packer, Marcham, 1965.    [4] *Lambeth 1958*, ii, p. 43.

# X

## THE RELATIONSHIP OF A UNITED CHURCH WITH OTHER CHURCHES

HERE AGAIN the experience of South India is valuable. At first, the idea was that the other Churches there would become part of the Anglican Church in India. That was seen to be impossible, and the Lambeth Conference of 1930 recognized this. "The united Church in South India will not itself be an Anglican Church: it will be a distinct Province of the Universal Church."[2] While C.S.I. "desires to be permanently in full communion and fellowship with all the Churches with which its constituent groups have had such communion and fellowship",[1] it insists that it "claims the right to be free in all spiritual matters from the direction or interposition of any civil government. It is an autonomous Church, and free from any control, legal or otherwise, of any Church or society external to itself".[3] This kind of claim is made in all Schemes for a united Church, together with the same desire for continuance and widening of fellowship with Christians everywhere.

Similarly, from the side of the Church of South India there is complete freedom for all its ministers and members to accept whatever fellowship is offered to them by other Churches, while it is fully recognized that C.S.I. cannot determine what must rest with those other Churches to settle.[4] In fact, all the parent Churches other than the Anglican have welcomed members and ministers of C.S.I. to an unrestricted participation in their life, as guests from a sister Church and as one in Christ. Plainly, however, if someone from C.S.I. wishes permanently to become a member of a Church elsewhere, he must accept the discipline of that Church in its fullness.[5] So also it is clearly

[1] Quoted in *Lambeth 1948*, p. 42 (part ii). Cf. Sundkler, p. 218.
[2] *C*, pp. 12 f.
[3] *C*, p. 15.
[4] *C*, pp. 13 f.
[5] *BU*, p. 84.

recognized that ordination in the Church of South India confers on the minister no right to demand appointment to a charge elsewhere. For example, Methodist ministers ordained within the Methodist Church in South India were received into full connexion by the Methodist Conference in England, with all that that implied. This is not true of the present ministers of the Church of South India.

For Anglicans the matter is one for determination by each Province. All are agreed in making a distinction between ministers who have been episcopally ordained and those who have not, so far as permission to celebrate communion in Anglican churches for Anglicans is concerned. Most welcome communicants of C.S.I. to receive communion with them as visitors cut off from their own Church. In Scotland, the Episcopal Church requires an undertaking not to receive communion in a Church of any other denomination in Scotland. They must also have received episcopal confirmation. This same requirement of episcopal confirmation is found in the Anglican Church in U.S.A. It is there curiously illogical, as bishops and presbyters episcopally ordained within C.S.I. are allowed to celebrate communion—and therefore presumably to receive communion—although not all of them will have received episcopal confirmation.

This leads on to another limitation on full fellowship, which first appeared in the Convocation resolutions passed in England in 1950. It was strongly asserted, both in the Report of the Joint Committee and at the highest level, that the insistence that bishops and presbyters of C.S.I. might only celebrate Holy Communion in churches of the Church of England if they undertook not to celebrate in other churches while in England was not an assertion of theological principle but a pastoral necessity in the circumstances of England.[1] In fact there has been a tendency to elevate it into a basic principle of action. It was followed in U.S.A., though there the boundaries are not national but diocesan. Fortunately, both Japan and Canada have imposed no such limitations. To many Anglicans it does not seem clear that to compel ministers of C.S.I. to deny in act the full fellowship which they have enjoyed from the first with other Churches, in order to gain a limited fellowship with Anglicans, is in fact to refuse them fellowship. The Synod Executive early on made it plain that, while not forbidding any who felt able conscientiously to do so to give such an undertaking and while recognizing that some, particularly missionaries of Anglican Societies while on furlough, might be in a special position, it could not

[1] *Church of South India, 1950*, pp. 22–24. Bell, *Documents, 1948–1957*, pp. 189 ff.

recommend the acceptance of fellowship on these terms. At present, the great majority of the ministers of C.S.I. have passed a sizeable part of their lives within one of the separate Churches now united in C.S.I. and it is obvious that those who were not originally Anglicans cannot be expected to cut themselves off from what are their parent Churches. But, increasingly, the past becomes irrelevant in this separating form, as men and women who have never known the previous disunity grow up and take responsibility in the life of the Church. The first bishops whose whole ministry has been within C.S.I. are already in office. They cannot be expected to seek fellowship with Anglicans at the cost of refusing a freely given fellowship with other Christians to whom C.S.I. owes no less a debt of gratitude.

The importance of this is that, unless Anglicans everywhere are ready to think again and to drop this attempt to make the members or ministers of a united Church choose to have fellowship *either* with Anglicans *or* with other Churches, no rite of unification will in fact result in real fellowship for the whole of a united Church with the Anglican Churches. Anglicans made up 50 per cent of the original membership of C.S.I. In some other areas they are only a small proportion and therefore there will be little effective fellowship with Anglicans unless there is a change in this requirement. Anglicans—and especially members of the Church of England—are inclined to exaggerate their own importance and numbers. Why, for example, should they imagine that Methodists, when they enter into a united Church, will agree to cut themselves off from a far larger world fellowship to satisfy the scruples of some, though not all, Anglicans?

A further question which needs careful consideration is that of the relationship of a united Church to the World Denominational organizations. In the 1929 Edition of the Scheme, the hope was expressed that C.S.I. would be in full communion with all the parent Churches, "that its bishops would be invited to the Lambeth Conference and that delegates would attend the World Presbyterian Conference, the World Union of Congregational Churches and the Ecumenical Methodist Conference".[1] This does not appear in the present Constitution. No invitation has been given by the Lambeth Conference, which has remained a purely Anglican gathering. There is, however, a recognition by the Lambeth Conference of 1958 that changing circumstances and the increasing number of united Churches, with a corresponding decline in the area of denominational Anglicanism, call for a change of

[1] Sundkler, p. 171.

policy.[1] A meeting of the "Wider Episcopal Fellowship" has already been held, at which C.S.I. was represented. It has not yet been decided whether bishops of united Churches shall be invited to attend the next Lambeth Conference as members. The other World Denominational bodies concerned have invited C.S.I. to send delegates to their meetings. The matter was given careful consideration and the policy adopted by C.S.I. is that it cannot accept full membership of bodies which are in their constitution denominational, for that might involve its representatives in decisions which spring from the common acceptance of certain denominational principles, which are not those of C.S.I., and might seem to bind C.S.I. to accept them. It is ready to send fraternal delegates to take the fullest possible part in all the deliberations of such bodies.

This is one aspect of a more general truth, which many in the old denominational Churches find it very hard to grasp. They look upon denominationalism as the normal state of Christians, and of those who have passed on into a greater measure of unity as in some sense still belonging to their previous denomination, still thinking along the old lines and bound by the old rules and loyalties. They find it difficult, if not impossible, to grasp that a return to denominationalism, should change of residence make that necessary, is not a coming back home but an experience deeply painful and frustrating. It involves again the acceptance of limitations which had become obsolete and of assumptions no longer valid. It brings a cutting off of fellowship with other Christians which has been immensely enriching. It seems to call for readiness to defend denominational loyalties which no longer correspond to reality. Unity is not a minor adjustment which leaves the foundations unshaken. It permeates all thinking and living. The denominationalist will inevitably find the Christian who has experienced even a partial unity unreliable. Where disunity still reigns, so much of the time, energy and material resources of any denomination are taken up with keeping the denominational machine running. There are a vast number of vested interests which make any radical change difficult, however devoted and admirable the individuals concerned may be. Every fresh organization and every new institution make it harder to move towards a real unity, in which the existing denominations will die in order that God may create something new and nearer our Lord's prayer. Few people really welcome drastic changes, and many unconsciously hope that the denominational structure within which they

[1] *Lambeth 1958*, i, p. 35; ii, pp. 24 f.

have come to know God and to which they have given their service will last their time. There is, in the West, a curious unawareness of the speed of change in many parts of the world, a speed of change which cannot pass the Churches by.

It is for this reason that final decisions about Plans for unity must be taken where the union will happen, for only there are the realities of the situation inescapable. There God's will must be obeyed, and there the price of that obedience must be paid, by God's people in that place. Upon them rests the immediate responsibility for confessing Christ intelligibly and relevantly, by the quality of their corporate no less than of their individual life, to the world in which they are set. The misguided attempts to gain from Churches elsewhere an assurance of full fellowship and communion before the decision to unite has been taken, made by the Anglicans about Ceylon and North India/Pakistan, have resulted in a frustrating incoherence. In the words of Bishop Roseveare from Ghana, "It is unlikely that any part of the Anglican Communion negotiating for reunion will ever repeat that ghastly mistake."[1] Union can never be easy, if it is the kind of unity for which Christ prayed. It cannot be reached without suffering. There is no way forward if you insist on keeping open a way back.

The Nigerian Christians asked Bishop Sumitra, "What has the united Church gained? and lost?" He answered, "Is it right to do a profit and loss account when it is a question of trying to be obedient to the Lord's will? We have tried to be obedient. We have lost some friends and supporters. We have lost some financial support. We believe we did right and we are happy. But our gain by far outweighs our losses . . . gain or loss we have the joy of having obeyed the Lord."

[1] Article in *Theology*, August 1965, p. 375.

# INDEX

## (A) PERSONS

## (B) SUBJECTS

(Where a subject is sufficiently indicated by a chapter heading, it is not
separately listed here)

## (C) CHURCH OF SOUTH INDIA (C.S.I.)